HOW TO AFFORD A HUSBAND

HOW TO AFFORD A HUSBAND

or any other live-in lover

JUSTINE DAVIES

ABC
Books

Published by ABC Books for the
AUSTRALIAN BROADCASTING CORPORATION
GPO Box 9994 Sydney NSW 2001

Copyright © Justine Davies 2009

First published March 2009

ISBN 978 0 7333 2390 4

Designed by Christabella Designs
Set in 11.5/15pt Bembo by Kirby Jones

General Advice

The information in this book contains general information only. It does not constitute individual financial advice and should not be relied upon as a substitute for individual professional advice. Being general advice, the information does not take into account the individual situation or particular needs of any particular person. The information is correct at the time of writing, based on current 2009 legislation, but may be subject to change.

CONTENTS

INTRODUCTION

You only live once, but if you do it right,
once is enough.
Mae West

Despite the 'Husband' bit of the title, this book is intended for anyone in the process or about to start the process of sharing finances with someone else. Whether you are in the throes of rosy-eyed infatuation and are about to move in together, are in the middle of choosing bomboniere for the wedding tables, or are simply wondering why your partner seems to think that farting in bed is okay just because you have been living together for more than 12 months, this book is for you.

Making a commitment to someone, whether getting engaged, getting married or moving in together, is a huge step. Being 'in love' is just a small part of it. Partnership indicates a willingness to share time together—both good and bad—to share friends, family and experiences, to grow together as a couple. Maybe even start a family down the track. It also usually indicates a willingness to share finances.

While all the emotional aspects of cohabitation are covered very well in numerous books and articles, there is sometimes a lack of detailed information on sharing money. Yet survey results reveal that finances are consistently listed as a cause of conflict between couples. Surely it's a topic deserving of public debate?

It's not a sexy topic, though; very few of us really enjoy thinking about finances. And certainly not when there are far more exciting things to do, like house-hunting, choosing furniture, changing jobs, shopping, dining out and indulging in sports and hobbies. Let's face it, when the man (or woman) of your dreams is whispering sweet nothings in your ear, you really do want them to be sweet nothings and not a discourse on the day's expenditure.

On the flipside, you do want those sweet nothings to continue forever after. Financial stress doesn't just create money problems; it also helps to create other forms of relationship stress as you both work harder and longer to earn more, trying vainly to get ahead. It can impact on the quality of time you have to spend together and also affect your enjoyment of that time. When you consider that more than one in three marriages in Australia ends in divorce, let alone how many relationships don't make it to the marriage stage before foundering, it stands to reason that there are a lot of people who can't deal with the financial aspect of living together. Generally, it's because they haven't been shown how.

Take myself as a case in point: when my boyfriend (now husband) and I first moved in together about 15 years ago, I had absolutely no idea about managing joint finances. Prior to that my only experiences were living at home and living in share houses. Never sharing money. When Cameron and I set up house we pooled all our income, but the stress of paying rent, bills, other expenses and trying to save for a house deposit was overwhelming. My salary was paid fortnightly and generally the money was gone by the end of the first week. I could never work out exactly where it went. A couple of late nights here, some new clothes there and half a tank of petrol (there wasn't enough money left for a full tank). The empty pantry was good for the figure, but the empty bank account usually led to bickering and (on my part) tears.

The bickering is understandable. Your attitude to money and the way that you handle money is a product of your upbringing and the way that your parents handled money, as well as your education, your observation of the way friends and colleagues handle money along with a bit of your own unique personality thrown into the mix. Your partner has had a different upbringing and education/social influences, not to mention having their own unique personality, so it stands to reason that their attitude to and handling of money is going to be different from yours. Not necessarily better or worse, just different.

Compromise, not dictatorship, is the way to go. Just as you can agree to compromise on where you live, what you eat and who you spend time with, you can also compromise on how you handle your joint finances.

Studies have shown that mega-rich people do not have higher levels of happiness than the (financially) average person. So winning lotto will not make a difference to your wellbeing. It is the day-to-day handling of the money that you *do* have that could be the make or break for your relationship.

As a financial planner I have seen clients at all stages of life, from school leavers to the long retired. I love dealing with newly married or newly partnered clients—they are usually happy with life, happy with each other and full of big plans for the future. It is the people who are financially organised who tend to stay happy over the years.

It doesn't take a lot of effort to be financially organised once you know the basics. And once you have the systems in place it takes very little time to maintain. And anything that leaves more time for cuddling, having incredible sex, staring intently into each other's eyes or ... oh, what the heck, just watching television, has to be a good thing.

I will take you, chapter by chapter, through the main building blocks of financial security (aka The Main Things You Need To Know). The last few chapters will cover specific situations that may or may not apply to your life.

The book is designed to be read from start to finish (no skipping of chapters). For the first six chapters, at least, it's best to actually follow the suggestions in each particular chapter before moving on to the next one. That way, approaching your finances won't seem too overwhelming.

The strategies in this book apply just as much to males as females. It would be great to encourage your partner to read the book as well. The information here also applies to same-sex couples—it's for anyone who is sharing finances. For ease of writing I am assuming that the reader is she, the partner is he, and everyone else is they. Good luck!

CHAPTER 1

GETTING ALONG

Have dinner ready. Plan ahead, even the night before, to have a delicious meal ready, on time for his return. This is a way of letting him know that you have been thinking about him and are concerned about his needs. Most men are hungry when they come home and the prospect of a good meal (especially his favourite dish) is part of the warm welcome needed.

The Good Wife's Guide*

---

* The quote above (and at the start of most of the succeeding chapters) is attributed to an article published in a US-based magazine, *Housekeeping Monthly*, in May 1955. There is some debate about whether the magazine ever existed, but the good wife 'tips' provide some amusement. Apparently someone thought they were worthy of transcribing and publicising—even if they weren't quite courageous enough to put their name to it.

Oh yes indeed, planning the evening dinner is absolutely at the top of my 'to do' list all day—not! Having said that, I do enjoy cooking. I like donning the apron, getting out the recipe book and creating a masterpiece. I couldn't care less whether I get to eat it— all the fun is in the creating.

Or usually it is.

Have you heard the expression 'too many cooks spoil the broth'? In my opinion, anything more than one is too many cooks. I don't mind which one of us is doing the cooking—my husband or myself—but there's only room for one of us in the kitchen.

Or one of us outside, of course. Apparently something like 97 per cent of Australians own a barbecue and 85 per cent prefer cooking on the barbecue rather than indoors. Interestingly, very few women are allowed (or want) to use the aforementioned barbecue. Why is that? What is it about the barbecue that brings out the inner chef in men who may not set a willing foot in the kitchen from one year to the next? '[Men find it] so popular because it brings cooking back to basics—just a grill plate, a pair of tongs, raw meat and flame,' says Australian food writer Allan Campion. 'Blokes love nothing more than standing around the BBQ, drink in hand, ribbing each other how they could do it better if only they were in charge of the tongs. Typical male behaviour many would say!' And even if your man really can't tell the difference between a lamb chop and a T-bone steak, Allan cautions that taking over the tongs can be akin to declaring war. 'BBQ tongs are like the TV remote control of the backyard,' he explains, 'so whoever holds the tongs holds the power ... they should never be handed over lightly.'

And even if your husband's individual cooking style is not exactly to your taste, I can't imagine there would be too many complaints. After all, any dinner that someone else cooks is a good dinner!

Speaking of individual styles…

Financial Tip of the Week
Remember that you are two individuals.

I have already covered this briefly in the Introduction, but it's worth spending a chapter reiterating it because it can be a major reason for financial conflict between couples. Repeat after me—'You are two individual people. You have separate goals, values, convictions, assumptions and attitudes towards money. You cannot expect to automatically manage money in the same way.'

It's stating the obvious to say that you and your partner are different, but so many people overlook this fact when it comes to finance. You don't always expect to have the same taste in clothes, movies, books, music or hobbies as your partner—their contrast is probably one of the things that attracted you to them in the first place. Yet many people automatically expect to have the same priorities and habits when it comes to managing money.

Living day-to-day and assuming it will all work out in the end might be your partner's preferred financial strategy, whereas planning things carefully and sticking to a budget might be your instinct. Each is going to feel very uncomfortable if forced to strictly follow the other's regime. This applies equally, by the way, to the other aspects of your life together as well as to money.

It may not even be about how to manage money; it may simply be about what to spend the money on. Clothes, holidays and fun times together might be all-important to you, whereas sacrificing those things to pay extra off the mortgage might be all-important to your partner. Does this make either of you wrong? No. You just have different mindsets. And again, each of you would feel uncomfortable (not to mention resentful) if forced to completely abide by the rules of the other.

The above differences don't matter at all when you are living separate lives and managing separate finances. It's only when you decide to share your life together, with all the associated implications, that financial habits you once viewed as an endearing trait in your beloved can become a major sticking point.

So what is it that makes our respective attitudes different? In short, our life experiences. Family is a huge influence on our attitudes in so many areas, and one of those areas is money. How your parents managed money and their attitudes to money and investments will have had a significant impact on your subconscious. If you came from a family where saving money was valued to the detriment of family enjoyment, as a result of this you may now be determined to make each day happier by fulfilling all of your short-term consumer wants. If you came from a family where there was tension because of lack of money or mismanagement of money, you may now be determined to ensure that you have plenty of money set aside for a rainy day so that you will never end up in debt. If you came from a family where money was plentiful and your desires were all satisfied, you may have grown into adulthood expecting all of your desires to be fulfilled with little effort on your behalf.

These are only a few scenarios. You will know what your own upbringing was like and what impact it may have had on your current attitudes.

> In the husband's family, the father may have been the breadwinner but the mother may have done all the day-to-day finances, so the husband naturally assumes that his wife will be able to take on this role. But in the wife's family it may have been her father who always dealt with the money and he may not have talked about it with his kids, so in fact she doesn't know how to go about managing day-to-day finances and assumes that her husband will automatically do it. If they don't sit down and talk about their expectations, they can be in financial crisis before they realise what the problem is.
>
> —*Lola Mashado, Venue Manager, Relationships Australia*

Friends and colleagues can also influence our attitude towards money, either by peer pressure or simply by our own unconscious imitation. If most of your friends are single with no commitments and have a healthy disposable income, then they (and you) may enjoy a pretty self-indulgent lifestyle. And there's nothing wrong with that. Likewise if your colleagues are given to long lunches and luxurious shopping expeditions you won't want to be the odd woman out, and will probably spend accordingly.

Media can also play a role in our attitudes. We are constantly bombarded via TV, billboards, the internet and mobile phones with advertisements for consumer goods. There is so much stuff out there to buy, all containing the subtle message that you *need* this particular product. We are also bombarded with advertisements from personal finance companies reassuring us just how easy it is to get a loan, not to mention the reams of unsolicited credit card pre-approvals that arrive in the letterbox. It can be difficult to refuse all those enticements.

Ask yourself the following questions:

- What was my parents' attitude towards money when I was growing up?
- What are the overriding attitudes of other influential people in my life towards money?
- Has my working environment shaped my attitude towards money?
- What other things shape my attitude towards money?
- How would I describe my own attitude towards money? What makes money important for me?

Now think about your partner. He hasn't had the same life experiences as you—he has had his own set of different experiences that have shaped his attitudes just as yours have been shaped. Ask him to answer the questions listed above as well. For a more detailed questionnaire, try Appendix 1 on page 211. Then compare your answers—there will almost certainly be areas of difference.

Difference can be a good thing. If a couple is too similar

in their instinctive attitudes they run the risk of developing financial tunnel-vision; of never stepping outside their comfort zone to try something different. While this sameness may make for less day-to-day conflict, it can cause just as many long-term problems in the form of missed opportunities. Celebrate your differences. After all, that's what attracted you to each other in the first place.

All very well, you may be thinking, but you still have to live together day to day. Quite right, and the answer to that is COMPROMISE and COMMUNICATE. Just as in every other facet of your life together, you both (the important word there is *both*!) need to compromise and communicate in order to live happily ever after. After all, the object of this book isn't to change your beliefs about money, it's simply to make you aware of them and to learn how to join forces to successfully manage money as equal partners.

> Communication is the key to resolving conflict. Without regular, honest communication the underlying causes of the conflict cannot be addressed and resolved. Talking about money attitudes should happen as early as possible in a relationship. People talk about all sorts of other things, like having kids, career aspirations, home ownership. But they don't talk about their attitudes to money.
> —*Lola Mashado*

Keep these words in mind as you work your way through the chapters—*compromise* and *communicate*. You are not 100 per cent right and your partner is not 100 per cent right but you can be 100 per cent right together.

CHAPTER TWO

YOUR CURRENT SITUATION

Prepare yourself. Take 15 minutes to rest
so you'll be refreshed when he arrives.
Touch up your make-up, put a ribbon in your
hair and be fresh-looking. He has just been
with a lot of work-weary people.
The Good Wife's Guide

As sexist and archaic as the above statement sounds there is an underlying truth in the advice. At some point in every relationship the rose-tinted glasses come off and we give our partners a slightly more objective appraisal. It is at this point that staying 'in love' can require a little bit more effort.

It's easy enough to start with, when everything in your relationship is new and exciting. How hard can it be to be in love with someone who takes you out for dinner, listens attentively to everything you say, compliments you on your clothes and tells you how wonderful you are? What's not to love?

Down the track, as that initial and intense period of new romance wanes, you may find it slightly more difficult to stay 'in love' with someone who never stacks the dishwasher, goes glassy-eyed while you're talking to them and doesn't notice what you are wearing.

Later still you are gritting your teeth and resolutely remaining 'in love' with someone who is developing a beer belly, thinks takeaway is a treat, farts while watching TV and reads the paper while you're talking. You can't remember the last time he gave you a compliment—although come to think of it, you probably haven't paid him much attention lately either. Get the picture?

Not that I want to make it sound like doom and gloom because, of course, it's not. But there is no doubt that romantically staying 'in love' forever requires a certain amount of commitment and persistence. Whether or not putting a ribbon in your hair is going to help is debatable but perhaps some other form of attire might.

Financial Tip of the Week
Map your current situation.

In addition to ensuring that you take care of your current romantic situation, to keep it alive and well, you also need to ensure that you are on top of your current financial situation, to keep it alive and well. By 'current financial situation' I mean your assets and liabilities—what you OWN and what you OWE. In order to make any sort of financial progress in life you need to know what your starting point is and that involves making a list of what you currently own and a list of what you currently owe. It sounds pretty simple, doesn't it? Let's do it.

Get a piece of paper and rule a line down the middle of it. Write 'Assets' at the top of the first half and 'Liabilities' at the top of the other. Basically, assets are things that you own and liabilities are things that you owe. Appendix 2 on page 212 is a balance sheet, listing the most common assets and liabilities. Use this as a template for your situation but remember to add any other assets you may have that are not listed and subtract any other liabilities. If you and your partner don't yet share finances you may prefer to do one of these each, or otherwise just add them all together as shown below.

Let's get started. Your balance sheet may look something like this.

ASSETS	OWNER	$ VALUE
House	Joint	335,000
Contents	Joint	15,000
Bank account	You	2,000
Bank account	Partner	3,000
Shares	You	10,000
Managed fund	Partner	4,000
Artworks	Joint	8,000
Car	You	7,000
Car	Partner	15,000
Superannuation	You	10,000
Superannuation	Partner	10,000
Total		**$419,000**

LIABILITIES	OWNER	$ VALUE
Mortgage	Joint	240,000
Visa card	You	5,000
Mastercard	Partner	1,500
Store card	Joint	1,500
Car loan	Partner	8,000
HECS debt	You	2,500
Total		**$258,500**

Other assets may include investment properties, boats, caravans, endowment policies (insurance policies that have a savings component), term deposits, share of a business, loans you have given to another person. Other liabilities might include personal loans, tax bill, an overdraft account, an investment loan, to name a few. To find out your net worth you simply subtract your liabilities from your assets. So in the example above, subtract $258,500 from $402,000 (equals $143,500).

Of course, your individual situation may be quite different from the one above. You may both be just starting out on your working life and not have anything much in the way of assets at this stage. Go through this exercise anyway. Even if your total combined assets are slightly less than a weekly grocery bill and you have no debts, it is still important to commit it all to paper. And don't overlook items such as superannuation. Just because this is usually out of sight doesn't mean it should be out of mind.

When you go through this exercise make sure that you are thorough. Don't conveniently 'forget' the Visa card that you owe $1000 on (don't let your partner forget it either).

And make sure that any value you add in for items such as collectables or jewellery is realistic—a fire-sale value can be very different from an insured value. The same applies to the value you estimate for other discretionary items such as your home, cars, etc. Obviously items such as bank accounts and shares have a (reasonably) set value and are much easier to estimate.

It's a shame that we can't add intangibles onto the balance sheet. An American/British study of 16,000 Americans titled 'Money, Sex and Happiness' (what a great job those researchers must have) found that couples who have sex at least four times per month effectively create happiness worth US$50,000 per annum. Apparently the Australian average for sex is three times per week. Using the US study as a base, that means that most Australian couples are 'earning' about US$162,000 per year in happiness. And some newlyweds may well be theoretical millionaires; if only all that happiness could be converted into cash!

Anyway, if you have done your balance sheet and are staring at a negative net worth (that is, you owe more than you own), well, it's not great but it's not the end of the world either. And it's *definitely* better for you both to know where you stand rather than avoiding the truth. Unless it is caused by something outside your control, such as a massive HECS debt, then what a negative net worth figure does mean is that you are living beyond your means. All very well for the first year or two that you do it, not so good later on when you have racked up large personal debts that you can't pay off. Better to get on top of them now.

Chapter 4 takes you through how to set up a kick-ass budget and Chapter 5 shows you how to track your expenses on a daily basis (riveting stuff, I know). Chapter 7 will provide you with strategies for getting rid of personal debt and Chapter 8 will put in place strategies to reduce your expenses. By the time you have gone through all this you will definitely have the ability to turn a negative-asset situation into a positive, with minimal pain.

There are so many fun and exciting and challenging things that you will want to do throughout your life. A lot of them will cost money. The sooner you and your partner master the basics of managing your money, the more likely it is that you will be able to do the things you want, without having to stress about the financial consequences.

CHAPTER THREE

YOUR FUTURE GOALS

Be a little gay and a little more interesting
for him. His boring day may need a lift and
one of your duties is to provide it.
The Good Wife's Guide

*While being a little gay may or may not appeal to you, it is nice
for both of you to have a mental lift at the end of a working day.
When you first fall in love it isn't hard to quicken each other's pulse
rate. Just being there is probably going to do it. Later on, though,
giving each other a 'mental lift' might need a bit more conscious
effort.*

*Of course, the things that might give you a mental lift could be
quite different from the things that will give your partner a mental
lift. Hence that pesky word we keep coming back to—compromise.
Perhaps romantic dinners with meaningful conversation in nice*

restaurants would keep the spark alive for you; perhaps he wants more, or different, sex. You may find that your 'lifts' can easily be combined for mutual benefit. For example, more romantic dinners and talking would probably and naturally lead to more and possibly different sex. And hopefully, more and different sex would naturally lead to more romantic dinners.

It can be a bit harder with mundane around-the-house stuff. After all, 'remembering to put out the garbage bins without being asked', offset against 'not talking to me when I'm watching TV', isn't quite as exciting or as much fun to achieve. It probably requires a greater level of forward planning and businesslike agreement than the dinner/sex example and probably needs a bit of dinner/sex reward thrown into the mix to keep the momentum going.

Financial Tip of the Week
Write down your 10-year goals.

Just as there are things that you could aspire to that could keep your relationship 'lifted', there are, no doubt, things that you aspire to that may increase your enjoyment of life. In other words, your goals. And the best way to start the process of achieving your goals is to write them down— make them real. Ideally, this is something for you and your partner to do together because you need to know that you are working towards the same goals, or at the very least are aware of what each other's goals happen to be.

It can be a lot of fun. Goals aren't set in concrete—a lot can change in 10 years—but it gives you a broad outline of the possibilities (and costs) that you may have over the next decade. There will always be things that crop up, like an overseas career or a ski holiday or (gulp) a pregnancy that you weren't expecting. At least if you have a 10-year plan that you are working towards, anything unexpected can be incorporated into it with a few other priorities shifted around, and it needn't be a financial disaster.

Having 10-year goals is about writing down those big one-off or irregular expenses that you plan to have. Things like small annual holidays or annual car expenses wouldn't get listed here. Instead they would be incorporated into your regular budget (we look at setting up a budget in the next chapter). Regular progression up the career ladder wouldn't go in here either (we take that into account in a later chapter on page 160), although the cost of postgraduate studies would. Spend some time doing this plan. Talk together about what you would like to do (remember the compromise principle), explore all the options and agree on what the most important things are—together.

You don't have to agree on every goal. You may not give a stuff about skiing and your partner may not give a stuff about savouring the wonders of the Italian countryside, but you can still acknowledge the importance of each to the other and happily work towards them together. Hopefully that sentence makes sense—I'm sure you know what I mean.

Okay, so when you do your 10-year plan, divide the goals into short term, medium term and long term.

Short term: 1 to 2 years
Medium term: 3 to 6 years
Long term: 7 to 10 years

Let's look at an example.

10-year plan

Time frame	Activity	Cost $
Short term	Overseas holiday	$5,000
	New car	$30,000
	Plasma screen	$5,000
Medium term	Buy house	$400,000 to $450,000
	Overseas holiday	$10,000
	Boat	$12,000
Long term	Start family – 1 year maternity leave	$50,000
	Buy investment property	$300,000 to $350,000
	New car	$45,000
	Another child – 1 year maternity leave	$50,000

This is a pretty straightforward example. There are lots of other things that could be added to the list, like paying for a wedding, more holidays, setting up your own business, moving overseas or interstate, putting a swimming pool in your backyard (definitely something on my list at the moment)— the possibilities are endless. Appendix 3 on page 213 is a blank template for you to use to list your own goals.

You won't always know what the cost of something is going to be, particularly for the bigger items, but you can probably make a pretty educated guess. At the end of the day the important thing is to estimate *something*—a ballpark figure, if you like. Writing a realistic cost next to each goal helps you realise that goals need to be achievable. Otherwise your plan could end up resembling a New Year's resolution list made while drunk—all very commendable but entirely useless.

Following on from that statement, there is no point in writing down dozens and dozens of expensive goals: you have to be realistic. The objective of this chapter is to make you think about your goals and to prioritise those goals in order of importance. Why list under short-term goals buying a sports car, buying a house, taking 12 months unpaid leave to do your Masters degree and a European holiday if you know damn well that your current financial position might just support a night at the movies and that's about it? Make the goals unrealistic and you run the risk of not achieving any of them because you are not focused on anything. Prioritise.

On the other hand, the objective here is not to stop you from having fun or to make you a miser with money. Don't leave the European holiday off the list altogether. Just work out where it needs to fit in the scheme of things. An Oprah Winfrey quote, 'You can have it all, you just can't have it all at once' sums this idea up very nicely.

Having said all of that we are not actually going to look at the 'how to' of financing your goals in this chapter; we will go through that in subsequent chapters. At the moment it's simply important to discuss your goals together, agree on them (or agree to disagree on some of them) and write them down.

And a quick pep talk. When doing this exercise (and every other personal exercise throughout this book), disregard the opinions of anyone other than you and your partner. These are YOUR goals—not the goals that your parents or friends or colleagues or anyone else thinks you should have—YOURS. You are the ones who will be living them and you are the ones who will be paying for them. So they should be what you want. You only get one life—make the most of it.

CHAPTER FOUR

DOING A BUDGET

Clear away the clutter. Make one last trip
through the main part of the house just before
your husband arrives. Gather up the
schoolbooks, toys, paper, etc., and then run a
dust cloth over the tables.
The Good Wife's Guide

OMG, it would be so good if someone would do that before I arrived home at night. Generally my breakfast cereal bowl is still on the table when I finish work, right where I left it 10 hours earlier. I think the above quote should be in a 'Good Husband's Guide', rather than a good wife's guide. It would be my observation that many men simply don't notice whether a house is clean or messy— how else could they survive in the pigsties they call 'bachelor pads'. Most women do notice the tidiness or otherwise of a house.

There was a survey done somewhere recently which stated that helping with the housework is far more likely to score men a bit of bedroom action than flowers or chocolates. If only men read those surveys!

Financial Tip of the Week
Do a budget.

If there was ever a survey of things that are *least* likely to result in a bit of bedroom action, doing a budget would surely rank up there as number one. It is tiresome and boring but, unfortunately, essential. In my opinion, a well-written budget is one of the most important foundations of future financial success. So, whatever else you do, persevere with this chapter as once it is successfully done every other chapter will flow on from it quite easily.

Consider this quote from financial guru Noel Whittaker:

Recently while giving a speech about investing, I mentioned the high cost of smoking and how much it reduced the money a person had to invest. Out of the left field came an interesting question: 'What you say seems logical, but the people I know who don't smoke seem to have no more money than those who do. Why is this?'

It was a great question, because it gave me the chance to explain why two people with similar incomes can end up more than a million dollars apart when they retire.

There is something in our psyche that encourages us to spend all we earn. Even though taxes were cut in July and everyone had more money in their pay packet, you can bet most have not invested those extra dollars.

The moment the increased pay packet arrived, they lifted their spending to use up the increase.

—*Noel Whittaker, article from* Smart Money 2007

Noel Whittaker is not the first to note that people usually spend what they earn. Writers have been commenting on that since money was first invented because basic human nature, by and large, hasn't really changed since that time. Cultures have, social customs have, the world around us has, but human nature stays the same. And most of us like to spend what we earn.

Why? Because most of us have far more wants than any amount of income is ever going to cover. Quite apart from the goals that we wrote down in Chapter 3, each of us has hundreds of little wants; things that we are convinced would make our life better in some way. Some of them might be as simple as a block of chocolate or a new pair of black shoes. Or maybe it's a new mobile phone; the one that does everything except cook dinner. And speaking of which, takeaway is a good option tonight; can't be bothered cooking.

The only way to prevent these wants from eating up every single dollar we earn is to do a written budget, to give ourselves a guideline on how much we can afford to spend on 'stuff', both big and small, each month.

Doing a budget can be an emotionally fraught activity. Unless you are both actuaries, which means it might be your idea of foreplay. If not, it may be a good idea to increase the intensity of all those spark-producing activities in the week leading up to this—to soften the financial blow—and to down a couple of quick shots of your spirit of choice before starting. Or perhaps just get your partner to down a couple of shots as it's a good idea for one of you to have all your wits about you.

In my experience only a small percentage of the population have a written budget. About 20 per cent, and of that 20 per cent the majority of budgets are completely unrealistic and hence completely useless. It is amazing what people will leave out of their budget or estimate tiny figures for. I have seen estimated clothing expenses of $200 per annum. Not per item, per annum. For goodness sake, what self-respecting couple spends $200 per annum between them on clothes? Gifts are often left out entirely. *Not* realistic, unless the couple doesn't have a social life at all. And speaking of a social life, entertainment expenses are often seriously underestimated.

These are just a few examples. Doing a budget is not about writing down what you would *like* your expenses to be. It is writing down what they *actually are*. Otherwise your budget is just another piece of paper.

Doing a budget is also *not* a blame game. It's not an excuse for criticising the spending habits of your partner. You and your partner are two different people and are going to have some different attitudes towards money and the management of money. Things that you think are important to spend money on may not be important to your partner and vice versa. Some of his spending excesses may shock you, and some of yours may shock him. But hey, what is a good relationship without a few surprises now and then?

So bite your tongue when doing your budget and don't offer any opinions on the wisdom (or not) of your partner's spending patterns. Remember—compromise. The same goes for him. Otherwise the whole exercise will disintegrate into a huge argument with no results.

If you think that it's genuinely beyond you to sit down together and do a budget then seek the help of a professional third party. Either a financial planner, if you have one, or a financial counsellor. To find contact details for financial counsellors that you could arrange an appointment with, check the website for the Australian Securities and Investments Commission (ASIC) <www.fido.gov.au>

Now that I have given you such a cheery view of budgeting, let's get on with it.

The more detail you have in your budget, the more accurate it will be. To do your budget properly you need three months' worth of bank statements; every statement for every account you have. Don't forget your credit card statements, store cards, your cheque account, your cash account, any savings accounts, online accounts, mortgage account, offset accounts. Everything. If you are missing a statement get a copy from your financial institution. If your statements are not sent out at least quarterly then print out a copy of the transactions online for the relevant time frame. Assemble all these statements, firstly into account order (to make sure you are not missing any), and then into date order.

Next you need a budget spreadsheet. Appendix 4 on page 214 is an example of a comprehensive budget. Either photocopy and use it or transfer the details into an Excel spreadsheet document. If there are expenses on the list that don't apply to you, cross them out. If there are any other expenses that you have that are not covered, add them in.

Personally, I think it is easiest to set the budget up as a computer document. That way you can save and file it and update it as your expenses change over time.

Now that you have your bank statements and your budget template you are just about ready to start. First, a quick explanation of the various budget categories.

Income is everything that you earn over the course of a year. Your wages/salary, commissions, bonuses, share dividends, interest on savings, regular overtime, government benefits and tax refunds. Whatever money you earn. With salary and so forth, list your after-tax income.

Fixed expenses are things that are, surprisingly enough, fixed. Expenses like mortgage repayment, rent, rates, utilities (gas, electricity, etc.), insurance premiums, petrol, car costs, groceries, subscriptions and memberships—you get the point, these are the expenses that don't change much. Even if the monthly amount varies, the yearly amount is pretty much predictable. These are expenses that are by and large necessary—like Christmas, tax and relatives, they are hard to avoid.

Regular expenses are like fixed expenses in that these are mostly necessary. However, to a certain extent, you can control the amount that you spend on these items—whether you spend a little or a lot is up to you. The monthly or yearly amount that you spend on each item can vary, although the overall cost of your regular expenses tends to stay the same year by year. One year it may be the furniture expense that wreaks havoc, the next year it could be the vet fees. Examples of regular expenses are clothing, home maintenance, appliances and medical expenses.

Discretionary expenses are something that you incur by choice. To a large extent, the amount that you spend on these items is entirely up to you. Examples are gifts, entertainment, hobbies. By saying that it is your choice to incur these expenses I don't mean that you shouldn't be spending money on them. You have to buy gifts. You have to go out. But whether you spend $20 or $200 is up to you.

This is the category that seems to cause the most conflict between couples. It goes back to that 'different attitudes' thing. Perhaps you spend more on clothes than your partner thinks is necessary. Perhaps he spends more on sport than you can imagine any sane person wanting to do. (Sorry about the really sexist example!) But you are both entitled to your different values and neither person's position is more valid than the other.

So we've gone through the theory; now let's put it into practice. Get your bank statements and your budget template and we'll start applying one to the other.

The way to do this is to go through each bank statement, line by line. Every single transaction on every statement—both credits and debits—should be able to go somewhere in your budget. It is up to you to remember what each transaction was for. Credit card and Eftpos are generally easy as the payee is listed beside the transaction. Cash withdrawals can be harder but three months should not be too long a time frame to stretch your memory over.

What do you usually spend your cash on? Try to be as accurate as you possibly can and keep in mind the CICO principle—crap in, crap out. With regards to cash spending, don't overlook small things like lunches and coffees, magazines, gift cards, car parking, after-work drinks. You should have a good idea of what you usually spend your money on.

Once you have been through each bank statement line by line, and have put all the information somewhere in the budget, have a quick look through it to see if there are any annual expenses that you have paid over the relevant three-month period. If so, divide the amount paid by four (there are four quarters to each year) and change the figure in your budget to that amount. So, for example, if you have paid your annual car registration of $400, divide this by four and put the $100 figure into your budget.

Next, multiply your budget totals by four.

Then have a think about any possible income that isn't listed on your budget yet. It may be something like a tax refund, commission, bonus and so forth. If there is anything you can think of, add it into your annual figures.

If there are any annual expenses that you haven't paid during the three-month period, work out what they are and put them into your budget.

Congratulations! You now have a pretty accurate picture of how much you earn and spend each year. Compare the 'how much you earn' figure with the 'how much you spend' figure. How does it look? Is it negative or positive? Don't worry too much if it's a negative figure, a lot of people do overspend and we will look at ways of reducing your expenses. The most important thing is simply to know the truth, otherwise how can you ever be prepared to do something about it? Ignorance might be bliss but knowledge is power.

Once you have finished the process, crack open a bottle of bubbly (or whatever is your relaxation method of choice) and take some time out. You've done a great job!

CHAPTER FIVE

TRACKING YOUR EXPENSES

Over the cooler months of the year you should prepare and light a fire for him to unwind by. Your husband will feel he has reached a haven of rest and order, and it will give you a lift too. After all, catering for his comfort will provide you with immense personal satisfaction.

The Good Wife's Guide

Fires are quite sexy really. The warmth, the flickering, the colour; even the sound and smell of a fire is somehow satisfying. They certainly provide the backdrop for numerous trysts in romantic novels: 'The tongues of flame licked around the upstanding logs, mirroring her tongue's action on his...' You get the point, I'm sure. Goodness knows how many fictional maidens have lost their virtue on a bearskin rug in front of a fireplace. According to the trashy romance novels, that is. Not that I spend my time reading trashy novels, of course. No, no, there are far more important financial things to do.

Speaking of which…

Financial Tip of the Week
Set up a tracking system.

Just one of those important financial things. The purpose of a tracking system is—to track your expenses. Bet you didn't see that one coming!

> You could have the best coach in the world, but unless you understand and apply the fundamentals, you'll never become a champion.
> —*Scott Pape, founder of* <www.barefootinvestor.com.au>

If your budget is the coach, the tracking system is the way that you apply the fundamentals. Often when people set up budgets they are quite unrealistic about how much they really do spend on things. For these people, a tracking system that tracks their real honest to goodness expenses highlights those areas where they are overspending compared to their budget.

A tracking system enables you to follow exactly how much you are spending, and on what, on a daily basis. The object of the exercise is twofold. Tracking your expenses means that you can, to a certain extent, *time* your expenses by controlling your discretionary spending (and here avoid running out of money before the next payday). Tracking your expenses also means that you can pinpoint areas in your budget where your expenses could be reduced.

So, from a timing point of view, keeping track of your expenses on a day-to-day basis gives you much greater control over your cash flow. As an example, if you know that you have already spent pretty much all of your entertainment money this week then you can maybe put off that dinner with friends until next week, after the next payday. That way you will still have money left in your bank account to put petrol in the car instead of having to resort to the trusty (and expensive) credit card to fund those necessities.

From a saving money point of view, tracking your expenses daily makes you far more aware of exactly how much you spend on what. Some spending categories that you have never thought about much can shock you with their significance. Common areas are gifts and clothing. Alcohol and entertainment can be big ones too. If you know exactly how much you have already spent in certain areas during the month you are far less likely to go out and impulse shop the following week.

So let's begin. The beauty of setting up your budget as a computer document is that it makes creating the tracking spreadsheet a 60-second operation. Simply copy and paste the budget template into a new file, delete the figures, call it something different (like 'tracking spreadsheet') and save it. Done! If you don't have a computer you can set up the same system in a paper journal from any stationary supplies shop. Simply start a new page for each expense and off you go.

Easy, right? All done. Well, almost … Your tracking system will only be useful to you if you are very diligent about putting in all of your earnings and expenditure. Preferably this should be done daily. It's the CICO principal again; if you don't put all your earnings and expenditure in accurately, as they occur, then all you will get is crap.

It is a task that you have to be really pedantic about: doing it daily is the best way to go. That way you won't forget the lotto ticket or the cappuccino or the DVD that you rented on the way home. All those little things can add up quite significantly. If you have internet banking it is easy to simply log on at the end of each day and check what amounts have been debited from your account. There are lots of things that you might have set up to come out automatically, such as gym fees, bank fees, health insurance and whatever else. These are all things that it can be very easy to overlook if you don't check them daily. Plus after a week or so the whole process will become second nature, and if done daily it should only take a couple of minutes.

Ideally you should keep doing this indefinitely but if you really struggle, set yourself a goal of tracking for at least three months.

You both need to have ownership of this process. Otherwise it becomes an exercise in nagging to try to find out exactly what was spent each day. No fun at all. So right at the start make an agreement that you will update your spreadsheet together after work each day or that one of you will make a habit of giving your spending information to the other each day. Whatever way you do the tracking, it needs to become a part of your everyday routine.

And, hard as it may be to believe, you will actually start to enjoy the process. Once it becomes an everyday habit, monitoring your expenses will give you a satisfying sense of power and control. No longer will you be running behind, vainly trying to get your income to catch up with your expenses. You will finally be in the driver's seat.

Have fun!

CHAPTER SIX

FACE YOUR DEBT

Do not deny your husband his indulgences.
After all, he is the one who earns the
money and it is his right to decide how
it should be spent.
The Good Wife's Guide

Actually, I made that one up. There were no money-related quotes at all in the Good Wife's article—I just couldn't resist adding one! Not that I'm advocating that point of view—far from it.

Having said that, we all work really hard, whether in paid employment, study or taking care of the kids and the house. I think that it's important for everyone to have some 'play money' to spend on whatever takes their fancy (within reason). After all, where's the fun in working hard if there are no rewards along the way?

Financial Tip of the Week
Attack your personal debt.

Of course it's important to balance the regular rewards with affordability. (I'm such a wet blanket, aren't I!) Otherwise where do most of us get extra money from when we're caught short? Our ever-present credit card, as it's such an attractive option.

And nowadays the credit card itself can be attractive too—financial institutions work their marketing departments overtime to come up with shapes, sizes and designs that the consuming public will hopefully find appealing. Silver, gold, platinum—whatever you like. Would you prefer a sports star, a hologram, or a discretely official-looking platinum card? How about one of each? Or a tiny one that you can wear on your necklace like a pendant? Cute. About $44 billion worth of cute.

Not at all cute though, when the credit card bill arrives in the mail. Oops, forgot about that purchase, and that one and that one. Damn that electricity bill, forgot the health insurance was being direct debited this month and I really must cancel that gym membership. What possessed me to buy that dress—it looks awful. Holy heck, look at that interest charge, not to mention the late payment fee.

Does that sound at all familiar? If not and you are a person who always pays the credit card off each month then you can probably skip this chapter. But if the above scenario sounds even vaguely like you or your partner, read on.

Using credit cards is fine. They are a handy tool for paying bills by phone, paying for restaurant meals, online purchases and holidays. They are a convenient way of keeping a record of itemised purchases and if you make use of the interest-free period and pay them off in full before interest starts accruing then they are a great cash flow tool as well.

But the benefits can come with some hefty costs attached. The interest for starters. The interest rate is likely to be well into the double digits and if you are not careful then the real cost of your purchase could end up being more than twice the amount you originally paid for the item. Literally. Try out the credit card calculator on the Australian Securities and Investments Commission (ASIC) consumer website <www.fido.asic.gov.au>. You can use this to work out how much interest you will pay on a particular debt at a particular interest rate over time. The results can be quite scary.

Another issue with credit cards is just how easy they are to use. It almost feels like it's your money rather than a personal loan. Unfortunately the bank doesn't see it (or charge it) that way. It's that old cliché—if you haven't had to earn something yourself then it can be hard to appreciate the true value of it. A credit card limit is something that you've not had to earn as the financial institution is only too happy to give it to you, which makes it difficult to see the credit card as being real money. You are far more likely to impulse buy with credit card money than with your hard-earned savings.

This can put you into a downward spiral, as having the credit limit handy means that you can spend more than you earn and over the months you get used to doing this. As you build up debt the interest charges become quite substantial and it then takes more of your earnings to pay the interest, let alone your usual costs. Then you have to rely even more on your credit card to pay your living expenses, and those interest charges become greater ... It's a vicious cycle.

So how do you break the cycle? Well, there are two issues that you need to address together. First, you need to do something constructive about the credit card balance that you currently owe. Second, you need to break your credit card spending habits.

YOUR CREDIT CARD BALANCE

Unless you are expecting a really large end-of-year bonus or a hefty tax refund then the chances of you paying off your outstanding personal debt in the short term are probably quite slim. Rather than trying to achieve the impossible and getting cross when you can't, accept that you have the debt and look at ways of reducing the financial impact that it has on you. In other words, minimise the cost of the debt.

The way to do this is to consolidate all your credit card/store card/other personal loan debt together at the lowest interest rate possible. Please note that I am not talking about debts that are a tax deduction to you, such as investment debt or potentially a car lease, I'm only focusing on your combined personal debts that have accumulated through overspending.

There are three main strategies that we can focus on to consolidate your personal debt and pay it off.

1. **Consolidate the debt into your mortgage**. If you
   have a mortgage then one option may be to incorporate
   your personal debts into your mortgage. Residential
   property has, by and large, increased in value over the last
   few years. Depending on when you bought your home
   you may well have some equity that you could use to
   your advantage. By incorporating your credit cards into
   your mortgage you will be paying interest on the debt at
   a much lower rate—and the same repayment levels will
   eventually pay off the balance.

   Let's look at an example.

Debt	Interest rate	Balance owing	Current monthly repayment
Visa	17%	$3,000	$60
Mastercard	16%	$2,000	$50
Personal line of credit	14%	$5,000	$100
Store card	21%	$1,500	$50
Mortgage – 25-year term	8%	$250,000	$1,931
Total		**$261,500**	**$2,191**

Assuming that you are able to consolidate your personal
debt into your mortgage the result would be as follows:

Debt	Interest rate	Balance owing	Current monthly repayment
Mortgage – 25-year term	8%	$261,500	$2,020
Total			**$2,020**

By consolidating your debts you will not only reduce your monthly repayments, but you will also (eventually) have your debt paid off. Alternatively you could keep your repayment amount the same ($2191 per month) and reduce the term of your home loan by five years.

Most financial institutions have home loan repayment calculators on their websites that you can use to calculate the figures for your specific situation. However, you should always speak to your banker before taking this course of action as there will be fees and charges associated with increasing your home loan.

2. **Consolidate your personal debts elsewhere.** Not everyone has a home loan to utilise, but it is still important to minimise the cost of your debt. Another way you do this is to simply consolidate all your credit cards and personal loans into one debt at the lowest possible cost. Some no-frills credit cards have interest rates that are only 1 or 2 per cent higher than a standard mortgage rate. Sure, you may not get interest-free periods or rewards points, but when you sit back and calculate how much those rewards points are really costing you, you may cheerfully wave them goodbye. Once you have found a suitable credit card then apply to roll your other balances in and calculate an appropriate level of repayment that will enable you to pay off the debt in a reasonable time frame.

Let's look at an example:

Debt	Interest rate	Balance owing	Minimum monthly repayment
Visa	17%	$3,000	$60
Mastercard	16%	$2,000	$50
Personal line of credit	14%	$5,000	$100
Store card	21%	$1,500	$50
Total		**$11,500**	**$260**

Assuming that the personal debt can be consolidated into a no frills credit card, the result would be as follows:

Debt	Interest rate	Balance owing	Minimum monthly repayment
No frills credit card	10%	$11,500	$230
Total			**$230**

The minimum monthly repayment would reduce by around $30 per month. However, by keeping the repayment level the same, at $260 per month, this would enable the debt to be paid out in approximately four years and nine months.

If you don't feel that you would have the discipline to pay off the outstanding balance unless forced to do so then an alternative would be to roll the various debts into one personal loan that has a fixed repayment and a fixed lifespan. Using the above example, you might set up a personal loan as follows:

Debt	Interest rate	Balance owing	Set monthly repayment
Personal loan – 5-year term	10%	$11,500	$247
Total			**$247**

In either situation the overall costs are not increasing but the debt is being paid off within a reasonably short time frame, rather than just making the minimum repayments over the long term. There is light at the end of the tunnel.

When searching for a credit card or personal loan your first port of call should be your financial institution. They can take you through the various options and any costs associated with each one. Otherwise you can do some research yourself. A good source of information is the CANNEX website <www.ratecity.com.au>. Just make sure that you read the small print on any products that you apply for to check for fees, charges or restrictive conditions.

There is more to a good credit card than simply the interest rate though, so it pays to do some other research. ASIC's consumer website <www.fido.gov.au> has some excellent general information about credit cards. Also check the Choice website <www.choice.com.au> for any recent credit card comparison reports.

Unfortunately consumers tend to compare credit cards based on the cards' interest rate only and many choose a card that has a low interest rate under the assumption that this will be cheaper option. In reality they could end up paying a lot more, depending on how the lender calculates interest. Additionally, a card that has a high interest rate but a long interest-free period could be a better option, depending on their spending habits.

—*Elise Davidson, spokesperson for Choice*

3. **Add the repayment of your debt to your short- or medium-term goals.** If for some reason you are unable to consolidate your debts onto a low interest rate, don't panic—we can still create light at the end of the tunnel. Keep making your minimum repayments as you currently do and pull out your list of goals that we created in Chapter 3. Add to your list of goals an extra goal called 'Repay Personal Debt'. It will depend on the size of your debt as to whether this should be a short-term or medium-term goal; you will need to make a judgement call on that.

Okay, so there are all the strategies for your current balance, but unless we also look at ways of changing your credit card spending habits then you will just be treading financial water.

YOUR SPENDING HABITS

Credit card spending habits can be very difficult to break because they may have crept up on you (or your partner) gradually over a number of years. It can take just as long to break the habits as it did to make them, so don't get too stressed if it doesn't happen overnight. Personally, I think that, like other addictions, going cold turkey is best. Give the following tips a try.

1. **Leave your credit card at home.** If you don't have the money with you, you can't spend it. Often the purchases we make on credit cards are impulse buys—things that we might think twice about if we were using cold, hard cash. Even details like grocery shopping; you are more likely to buy items that you don't really need if you pay by credit.
2. **Make good use of your budget and tracking spreadsheet to plan ahead for expenses.** We have already discussed this in Chapters 4 and 5. If you know accurately what expenses you have coming up over the next few weeks you can put money aside accordingly. This reduces the risk that you will be caught unaware and need to pay by credit card at the last moment.
3. **Avoid having expenses direct debited from your credit card.** It is too easy to forget about those expenses and not make provision for them in your actual cash flow. This means that the credit card balance will keep building up and up…
4. **Turn your credit card into a debit card.** If you know that you are going to pay an expense by credit card, make a vow not to do so unless you credit the money in first. That is, put the money into your credit card before you spend it.
5. **Use BPay instead.** A lot of your bills can be paid via internet banking. BPay is a fantastic tool because you

are using your own money instead of the financial institution's money.

6. **Pay all your important expenses as soon as you get paid.** By using your tracking spreadsheet you will have a fair idea of what expenses are coming up. As soon as you get paid, buy your groceries, put petrol in the car, pay any bills due that fortnight and buy any gifts needed that fortnight. That way if you are running out of cash by the end of the period then you will probably be able to tighten your belt, cut back on the discretionary spending and get by until next payday without relying on credit.

These are just some generic credit-avoidance tips—you will probably be able to think of plenty more that will apply to your specific situation. You are the best judge of your own character—you know what your weaknesses are, so find some strategies that will suit you and your partner and make a vow to stick to them. Don't get discouraged too quickly. These changes in your spending patterns are not going to happen overnight. Maybe write a DO NOT USE THE CREDIT CARD reminder and stick it somewhere you will see it every day. Don't worry too much if you have lapses now and then, at least you are on the right track.

CHAPTER SEVEN

STARTING TO SAVE

Minimise all noise. At the time of his
arrival eliminate all noise of the washer,
dryer or vacuum. Try to encourage the
children to be quiet.
The Good Wife's Guide

*One of the nicest things about being in a relationship is waking up
in the morning, rolling over and gazing at your beloved. True bliss.
One of the worst things about being in a relationship is waking at
2 a.m., rolling over and glaring at your beloved because he WON'T
STOP SNORING. Talk about minimising noise—not!*

*It might have seemed cute when you first started dating. After
all, it's not as though you were really wanting that much sleep back
then. His snoring may have seemed comforting; a solid, background
buzz to his warm bulk, making you feel protected and comforted.*

But after a few months of disturbed sleep, what was once cute may have become cringeworthy. Not so much a solid background buzz as a raspy chainsaw slicing through the wee hours of an otherwise peaceful night. Tense and on edge, each loud intake of breath may jangle your nerves like a monotonous car alarm or a persistent mosquito. Murders have been committed for less.

If this is your situation you are not alone. According to the American Academy of Otolaryngology (an otolaryngologist is another word for a snore doctor—imagine getting that word in a spelling bee!) around 45 per cent of adults snore and are more likely to be men than women. But help is at hand. There are over 300 different devices that you can buy to try to prevent the snoring. Your beloved could try a nasal strip or a dental plate. He could purchase the Snorben bi-lateral nasal insertion device (no, I did not make that name up), which looks like a rather kinky pair of handcuffs except that it's designed for the nose—nasal cuffs, I guess. Or you could admit defeat and buy some snore-blocking earplugs. Not really a sexy look, but then neither are panda eyes after a sleepless night.

Financial Tip of the Week
Start a savings plan.

What does a savings plan have to do with snoring? Nothing really except that, like snoring, a good savings plan should be constant and regular.

A savings plan is something that we all know we should have—it's one of those 'duh' type financial tips. But it's one thing knowing and another thing doing. Until you have been through the previous steps of setting up a budget and tracking system and controlling your credit cards then a savings plan is a really difficult thing to do properly. How can you save effectively if you don't know how much you need to spend? Now that you have your budget and your foolproof tracking system in place, a savings plan is the next item to tick off the list.

First, a quick pep talk. You *can* save money. Even if your budget is telling you that you currently spend more than you earn, you *can* save money. You just need a positive attitude and need to be willing to try.

You may be young DINKS, not-so-young parents of teenagers, mortgage-burdened thirty-somethings with toddlers, debt-free, child-free professionals or a combination of these. Irrespective, there will never be a better time for you to start saving than now. It may not be easy—there will always be more things that you want to buy than you have money for—but that's human nature, and that's life. Saving is about balancing your financial needs and your financial wants, and making sure there is something left over at the end of the day. And the key to saving is prioritising; the only way to save money is to put your savings at the top of the priority list. Technically there are two ways of saving. The first is to pay your expenses and then save whatever is left over. The second is to put away your savings first and then make your expenses fit into whatever is left. This second way—making your savings the first priority is definitely the way to go.

So how much should you save? Well, it depends on your 10-year goals (the ones you wrote down in Chapter 3). Irrespective of what your family situation is and what your goals are you should be able to save 10 per cent of your total net income. Everyone should aim to do that, at the very least. So if you bring home, say, $3000 between you each fortnight, you should be able to put at least $300 per fortnight into a savings account.

However, this 10 per cent is simply, as a minimum, what you should be able to save irrespective of your situation. What you actually *need* to save will depend upon the goals that you wrote down in Chapter 3.

Let's have another look at the example goals I wrote down in Chapter 3.

10-Year Plan

Time frame	Activity	Cost $
Short term	Overseas holiday	$5,000
	New car	$30,000
	Plasma screen	$5,000
	credit Card debt to pay off	$2,000
Medium term	Buy house	$400,000 to $450,000
	Overseas holiday	$10,000
	Boat	$12,000
Long term	Start family – 1 year maternity leave	$25,000
	Buy investment property	$300,000 to $350,000
	New car	$45,000
	Another child – 1 year maternity leave	$30,000

Quite a few goals. Your list may have more or fewer, depending on how specific you have been. You will see in the example above that I have also added a credit card debt (see Chapter 6) that needs to be paid off. Let's go through the list of goals line by line.

For the moment we are going to ignore the goals that you will be borrowing money to purchase (apart from any deposit needed). While the borrowings will have an impact on your budget, they are separate and distinct from your savings plan. In this chapter I just want you to get your head around (and get into the habit of) organising savings. We will look at your future borrowings later, in a separate chapter.

The first thing to do is get a highlighter pen and mark those expenses that you want to pay cash for (that means the expenses that you won't borrow money for). In my example, the holiday, plasma screen and credit card will be short-term cash expenses. A holiday and boat will be medium-term cash expenses and the two lots of maternity leave will be long-term cash expenses. In addition to these, you may need a lump sum of about $40,000 for the medium-term house deposit. Quite a bit of saving to achieve.

How do we work out how much needs to be saved per fortnight (or month, depending how you get paid) to achieve these goals? The easiest way is to add another column to the spreadsheet and calculate it out as follows:

10-Year Plan

Time frame	Activity	Cost $	Fortnightly savings (26 fortnights/ year)
Short term	Overseas holiday		
	– in approx. 12 months	$5,000	$5,000 / 26 = $192 per f/n
	New car	$30,000	
	Plasma screen		
	– in approx. 2 years	$5,000	$5,000 / 52 = $96 per f/n
	Credit card debt		
	– in approx. 18 months	$2,000	$2000 / 39 = $51 per f/n
Medium term	Buy house		
	– in approx. 4 years	$400,000 -$450,000	$40,000 deposit / $104 = $385 per f/n
	Overseas holiday		
	– in approx. 5 years	$10,000	$10,000 / 130 = $77 per f/n
	Boat – in approx. 5 years	$12,000	$12,000 / 130 = $92 per f/n
Long term	Start family		
	– 1 year maternity leave		
	– in 7 years	$25,000	$25,000 / 182 = $137 per f/n

Buy investment property	$300,000 to	
	$350,000	
New car	$45,000	
Another child		
– 1 year maternity leave		
– in 9 years	$30,000	$30,000 / 234 =
		$128 per f/n

Let's add up the savings we need to make. Ideally, we should be saving $1158 per fortnight in order to fund all the expenses in the example above. We might look at this figure and decide that it is unattainable, that it needs to be reduced. To do this, we need to reduce the goals. Perhaps the boat could be taken off the list—it's just wishful thinking rather than a must-have goal. Saving for maternity leave could be delayed, after all, there may be some benefit from the government and some benefit from your employer when you take leave. Perhaps saving for this could start once the short-term goals have been achieved.

Cutting out these items would reduce the fortnightly saving goal to $800. It's still a big stretch—that's $20,800 per year. But if the goals are to be achieved it has to be done.

That's how my example works. Now go through your own joint goals and follow the same process. Highlight the goals you want to pay cash for (and any house deposit that you want to save). Divide the cost of each goal by the number of fortnights that there are between now and when you want to spend the money (there are 26 fortnights to a year). Total them all up. How much do you need to save per fortnight to achieve all of your goals?

It probably seems like a lot of money however much the total is. Do you need to reassess your goals? Cut some of them out or lengthen the time frame? Doing this exercise is a fantastic way of working out what really are goals and what may be wishful thinking.

Once you have a final savings figure worked out you need to look at this in the context of what your income is and what your current expenses are. First, compare this savings figure to your income. What is your total combined after-tax income each year? What is your total annual savings amount that you have just identified? What does this savings amount represent as a percentage of your income? To work this out, divide your savings amount by your income amount. Let's pretend that in the example above it would be $20,800 divided by $100,000 = 20.8 per cent. Roughly 20 per cent of the combined income of you and your partner. For a double-income, no-kids couple this percentage should be achievable at a stretch. For others, it will depend entirely on your family situation. What is your percentage? Do you think it is a realistic amount? From my experience with clients I would suggest that 10 per cent should be achievable. Twenty per cent could probably be done with some effort. Anything above that will depend upon your family situation. Irrespective, if your savings goal is up around 40 per cent or 50 per cent of your net income then, unless you are somehow living rent and mortgage free on a large income, I would suggest this is going to be unrealistic and you should reassess your goals. You don't want to burn out too quickly through pushing yourself too hard.

You are doing well so let's keep going. We now need to compare this dollar amount of required savings to your current budget surplus (if you have one). Pull out your current budget that you did in Chapter 4. What is your total annual budget surplus (or deficit)? How does this compare with the amount of savings that you need to make?

It may be immediately apparent to you that you need to cut back your expenses a.s.a.p. if you are to have any hope of achieving your goals. Don't panic, it can probably be done. Divide the annual difference by 12 as this is the monthly amount of budget cuts that you need to make. Does it look like a realistic figure? Don't just say 'no' and throw the book away. Let's break it down into a bit more detail.

One of the reasons why it is so good to have your budget divided into different types of expenses—the fixed, regular and discretionary expenses—is that this enables you to pinpoint the expenses that you will likely be able to reduce to fit your savings into your overall plan. I'm talking, first up, about the discretionary expenses. That's where the quick hit will come from.

What sort of percentage is your savings shortfall compared to your discretionary expenses (divide your monthly savings shortfall by your monthly discretionary expenses)? Looking at the amount that you spend each month on discretionary expenses, do you instinctively feel that you would be able to cut these expenses by the amount of your savings shortfall? This isn't something that I can answer for you. If it is a savings goal that you do want to attempt, then it requires both you and your partner to agree and to be committed to it. If you are not working on your savings goals as a team then at least one of you is bound to end up frustrated and resentful—not something that you really want to encourage in your relationship.

Next step. You have worked out the fortnightly cost of your savings and decided that you will do your best to fit these savings into your budget. The savings have worked out to around 20 per cent (or whatever it is for you) of your after-tax income. What you must do now is set up a separate account for these savings to go into (either a mortgage offset account if you have a mortgage or an at-call savings account) and put in place a system for the money to be automatically transferred to this each fortnight on whatever day you get paid.

You could do this yourself via internet banking or, if your income is always a set amount, you could organise it as a direct debit, which means your savings will be squirrelled away on payday and hopefully it will be a case of out of sight, out of mind. From the remainder of your income you pay your fixed expenses, then your regular expenses, then your discretionary expenses, in that order. Doing it this way means that if you run short of cash before the end of the pay period it is on expenses that aren't really compulsory. You can forgo that skirt you saw in the shop the other day; you can't forgo the rent.

Sometimes you will have to pay a large fixed or regular expense, which means that you may be short of cash in a given week and you may need to fall back on your trusty credit card (they are a very handy thing to have for emergencies). But if you are using your tracking system to its full potential then these expenses should be incorporated into your overall budget and get paid off within a reasonable amount of time.

Don't fool yourself into thinking that you are saving if you are not. If you are putting $500 per month into a savings account but racking up an extra $500 of debt per month on the credit card then you are saving nothing at all, you are simply transferring money from one account to another.

I'm not trying to turn you into penny-pinching misers with no social life, and I certainly don't want you to stress about every dollar you spend on having fun. But you do need to be able to save for your goals, and by skimming your savings off the top as soon as you get paid and tracking your expenses regularly you should be able to make significant changes to your finances without any major changes to your day-to-day life.

Your savings plan will need to be reviewed on a fairly regular basis—roughly every 12 months. There are lots of reasons for this—your goals may change over time, as may the cost of your goals. Your income, too, will change over time. But once you have done the hard yards and set your savings plan up, reviewing it is a quick and easy task.

None of this is meant to sound bossy or condescending—my advice is based on both my professional experience and my own, often hard learned, often mistake-riddled personal experience. When I first left university and started work I was absolutely *crap* at managing money and remained crap at it for quite a few years. Sometimes I still am. Managing money is not something that anyone is born knowing how to do perfectly and nor will you ever become perfect. Hopefully you will achieve a greater sense of security.

A final quick word for this chapter—just put the money in an interest-earning cash account for the moment (or a mortgage offset account if you have a mortgage). There are numerous places that you could invest your money and we will take a general look at the main ones in a later chapter. The chief point of this chapter is to simply start saving.

CHAPTER EIGHT

CUTTING COSTS

Be happy to see him.
The Good Wife's Guide

Yes, well, it should probably be self-evident really. But there are always a few situations in which it's quite a challenge to be 'happy to see him'. They may, or may not, include:

- *When he bursts into the bathroom while you are having a shower to ask where his keys/wallet/car/brain is.*
- *When he arrives home halfway through a chick flick.*
- *When you are halfway through a girls' night out.*
- *At 3 a.m. when he phones to get a lift home because he doesn't have money left for a cab.*
- *At 3 a.m. when he's caught a cab home but forgotten his house keys and needs your help to navigate the doorway.*

Financial Tip of the Week
Start budgeting.

This means budgeting, as opposed to doing a budget. You have already done the latter and have been (probably) shocked by how much you spend. Since then, you have also set up a savings plan and organised to direct debit a set amount from your income each fortnight/month into a separate savings account. The only way this is going to be sustainable is if you now look for some ways to cut the expenses that are in your budget. That 3 a.m. cab fare is probably a really good place to start the cost-cutting exercise!

We face hundreds of spending options every single day. Some, like our mortgage or rent, are unavoidable. Some, like takeaway or a new pair of shoes, are impulse buys. Some are expensive, such as a bigger house, flashier car and better holiday destination. And some are cheap, such as a new DVD or a few 'extras' in the grocery shop. Don't let the size of the purchase fool you—often it is the small day-to-day stuff that is the quiet killer of the pay packet.

I have already mentioned in Chapter 7 that the 'quick hit' of cutting back your expenses is likely to come from your discretionary expenses, basically because these are the things that we don't always *have* to spend money on but enjoy spending money on.

Apart from these expenses there are a number of other areas where you can save money without cutting back your lifestyle too much.

Budget is not a dirty word! A budget is just a plan for your money. And planning ensures you are spending your money on the things that are important to you and not wasting it on the stuff you don't care about. Don't be afraid of your budget, it's just a simple tool that will empower you to live the life you dream of.

—*Cath Armstrong, founder of* <www.cheapskates.com.au>

The following are some examples of areas where it can be really easy to save money.

GROCERIES

Groceries are a fixed expense, right? Well, yes, but you might be surprised at how much of the money you spend on groceries is actually wasted money. A 2005 report: '10 Years of Recycling: The good, the bad and the ugly' by environment group Planet Ark found that Australians waste almost 3.3 million tonnes of food, both from buying things they didn't use and serving too much at the dinner table. That wastage translates into around $5.3 billion per annum—enough to feed the entire population of New Zealand for a year!

That is a lot of wasted food.

Apart from the food we waste, think about the food we buy. How often do you compare brands and prices? The store-branded product may be just as good but 20 per cent cheaper. The larger pack of washing powder may be much more economical than the smaller pack. The refill may be much cheaper (and better for the environment) than buying the entire product all over again.

There are a number of things you can do to reduce the amount you spend on groceries *and* reduce the amount of time you spend at the supermarket (which surely has to be a good thing).

- Once per fortnight, around payday, type up a dinner menu for the next two weeks. Allow yourself however many meals you would have with family and friends and fill in a suggested dinner for every other night. I know it sounds really anal, but it is an easy thing to do that helps you plan in advance and avoid having to dash to the shops several times a week.
- Use the menu you have just typed up as the basis of a shopping list to take to the supermarket. Don't forget to add in breakfast food, lunch food, snacks, fruit, bread, milk, pet food, toiletries and cleaning products. If you set the basics of your shopping list up on your computer and save it you will find that filling in the gaps only takes about five minutes each fortnight to do.
- Remember to take your shopping list with you!
- Put aside a set time each fortnight to buy the groceries.
- Compare brands. There is a big push by the large supermarket chains to fill the shelves with their own home branded product. Often the home brand is equivalent quality to the known brand, and may be significantly cheaper.

- Buy in bulk where practical—cuts of meat that can be frozen, cleaning products, dry pet food. The manufacturer saves on packaging when producing in bulk and passes the savings on to you.
- Buy refills.
- Keep an eye out for specials.

I know this all sounds incredibly boring, but it is much easier and much quicker to do your shopping this way than having to go to the shops every second day. You could potentially save 30 per cent on your grocery bill by doing this.

MORTGAGE

If you have a mortgage it is likely to be a significant part of your budget. It also may be something that you haven't reviewed for a while. But it's worthwhile reviewing it now and again to make sure you are getting the deal that suits you the best. As an example, a half a per cent reduction in interest rates on a $250,000 mortgage with a 25-year term could save you approximately $985 in repayments per annum.

There are a number of considerations with regards to your mortgage. The first relates to rates—should you be on a fixed or variable rate? That depends on what rates are currently doing, whether you want to make additional repayments and, importantly, how long you intend staying in your current residence. If you break a fixed rate term by moving house you could end up paying a financial penalty.

You also need to consider what type of loan suits you. Principle and interest is the most common, but there are also lines of credit, interest-only facilities and split facilities. I would suggest that a home mortgage should always be principle and interest repayments—forget about the more 'sophisticated' options unless your financial institution can suggest a very good reason for using them.

There are additional features that you can add to your mortgage, such as offset accounts (these are a fantastic idea), linked credit cards and mortgage insurance to name a few. Your financial institution will have a far more extensive list that they can go through with you.

If you already have a mortgage then your first phone call should be to your existing financial institution. They may well have a range of products or enhancements to your existing product that they can offer you very competitively. You can consider switching mortgage providers but keep in mind that the cost of doing so can outweigh the benefits gained.

Some online research can help boost your understanding of mortgages and what types are available. Try the CANNEX website <www.cannex.com.au>. The Australian Securities and Investments Commission (ASIC) consumer website <www.fido.gov.au> is also a great source of general information.

TELEPHONE

This is another fixed expense that we can potentially save money on. Most of us usually have several communication devices. A landline (or two or three), a mobile, an email address, internet access—we're all on call 24 hours a day and we cam to pay a fair bit for the privilege. It makes sense to ensure that you are getting a good deal.

Even with regards to your landline there is likely to be more than one competitor in your geographical location. For your mobile phone there will be dozens of competitors and for your internet service there may be hundreds. And then there are all the various packages that the providers have to choose from—complicated!

It is beyond the scope of this chapter to provide you with detailed information about what is available out there, but I can recommend some good websites to start your search from. Check out the following government Australian Communications and Media Authority (ACMA) website <www.acma.gov.au>. This contains guidelines on working out what services you need.

I am also a big fan of the Choice website for good information on just about any consumer product. Have a look at their website <www.choice.com.au>.

There are also lots of general tips on saving money on your phone bills. They include obvious things such as:

- Make calls to landlines from landlines rather than from mobiles.
- Take advantage of mobile to mobile deals that you have set up.
- Make long distance calls in off-peak times.
- Send a text message rather than make a phone call where practical.

- Send an email rather than phone where practical.
- Don't download crap onto your mobile that you don't really need.
- If you have a monthly download limit on your internet, try to pace yourself during the month to avoid exceeding the limit. Excess downloads can be expensive.

I'm sure that you can think of plenty more tips. When you take time to think about them they are commonsense really.

ELECTRICITY AND GAS

We're really on a roll here, aren't we? Here is another fixed expense that could potentially be reduced. Some states have privatised and deregulated their utility providers and some consumers now have a choice of provider. This isn't the same all over Australia, though. To check whether you are eligible for choice in your geographic location you will need to have a look on your relevant state government website. If you are eligible for choice, the suppliers should be listed on these websites (or links should be provided for the relevant websites). You can then compare the deals and packages that these suppliers offer.

Even if you don't have choice there are still a lot of ways you can reduce your energy expenses. Again, most of the state government websites or links have numerous energy saving tips that you can follow. They include things like:

- Using fluorescent light bulbs instead of regular ones.
- Turning off lights in rooms that you are not in.
- Turning off appliances you are not using at the wall switch.
- Only running your heating and air-conditioning when you are at home (and only when needed). Close doors to rooms that are not being used.
- Using natural ventilation where possible (open the window!).
- Minimising the use of energy guzzlers such as clothes dryers whenever possible.
- Installing roof insulation in your home. This is a big upfront cost but works out much cheaper in the long run.
- Using the cold water cycle on your washing machine.

Again, I'm sure that you can think of plenty more tips.

INSURANCE

I'll make a brief mention of the more common insurances here, being your home, contents, car and health insurance. More detailed information on insurance will be covered in a couple of later chapters.

There are so many different providers of these insurances that it can be a very complex thing to try to sift through all the different providers what they offer and what is included and excluded for variable costs. It can be worth doing the hard slog to make sure that what you have in place is the right type of cover for you, at a reasonable price.

There are a few general tips to get you started.

- With regards to home, contents and car insurance you may find that you can get a cheaper deal by packaging them all together under the one provider.
- Likewise if you have a mortgage, you may find that your financial institution offers a discount on insurance products purchased.
- Check the terms of your policy to make sure that everything you need to be covered is covered, but also check that you are not paying for extras that you are unlikely to use.
- The Choice website <www.choice.com.au> usually has some good comparisons of insurance providers available.
- With regards to health insurance, the government also has a great website <www.privatehealth.gov.au> that provides general information about private health and a comparison of the available funds.
- You could also use a health insurance broker such as iselect <www.iselect.com.au> or moneytime <www.moneytime.com.au> to select a cover, but keep in mind that most brokers only deal with a few of the available products on the market.

VEHICLE COSTS

Car costs are pretty much fixed. You have to get the car serviced, you have to put petrol in it. If it needs new tyres it needs new tyres. We have already mentioned car insurance. But how about the amount of use your car gets? Is it possible for you to share a car? Or to at least share the driving more than you do at the moment? Public transport can be inflexible, but it is worth considering. Could you save on petrol and parking costs (not to mention road rage) by catching a bus or train or tram instead?

MEDICAL COSTS

If you get sick you get sick, and there isn't much you can do about it, but make sure that you are registered for the Medicare safety net—*as a couple*. You are automatically registered as an individual, however, if you register as a couple then your medical expenses are added together and you will reach the threshold twice as quickly. What this means is that once you have incurred $1039 (the current threshold—please note it changes each year) of out-of-pocket medical expenses between you, Medicare will start paying 80 per cent of your additional medical expenses for out-of-hospital services rather than just the scheduled fee. You can check the details on the Medicare website <www.medicare.gov.au>.

CLOTHING

Of course you have to spend a certain amount of money on clothes each year, but try to minimise the number of worn-once-and-discarded items in your wardrobe. For me it is usually the impulse buys that end up at the back of the cupboard, never to see the light of day again (well, perhaps until a costume party). Have a plan before you go shopping and buy things that will match other things in your wardrobe. Sometimes it is better to spend more on a few really good quality items that will have lasting appeal rather than smaller amounts on lots of cheap and ultimately nasty items that you will regret later on.

BANK FEES

To an extent, with the amount of competition in the marketplace, some bank fees are an optional extra nowadays. Work out how much you are paying in fees each month on your various everyday and savings accounts and decide whether it would be worthwhile to switch accounts. Again, the CANNEX website <www.cannex.com.au> is a great source of information on all types of accounts and compares both the interest rates and the fees.

OTHER DISCRETIONARY SPENDING

You are the best person to work out ways of saving money on your discretionary spending as only the two of you know what your habits and preferences are. A few general tips are listed below to get you started.

- If you usually buy your lunch, start making it at home and taking it to work. A saving of even $6 per day over a 48-week working year is over $1400 in spare cash.
- Cut down the amount you spend on gifts by planning your purchases in advance rather than dashing out at the last moment. Also make use of craft and farmers markets for some great alternatives to the standard shop-bought fare.

- If you smoke, are you willing to stop? In the article I quoted at the beginning of Chapter 4, Noel Whittaker states that cutting out a one pack per day habit will save about $4000 per annum, which over 15 years in a good share portfolio could be about $175,000. It's great for your health too!
- Plan your holidays in advance to take advantage of any good value package deals that might be available.
- Are there things that you can buy second-hand without compromising on quality? You can buy just about anything through weekend newspapers, markets, garage sales and online sites such as ebay.
- Cut down on the amount of takeaway you have during the week. Making your lunches will help with this, as will doing up your fortnightly menu and shopping list discussed in Chapter 7. Your figure will also appreciate it!
- If you are a gambler, give yourself an absolute, definite dollar limit when you play your chance of choice. No swiping your card through the always available ATM for a bit more. Vow to yourself that when your limit is gone, it's gone.
- When you have a big night out, set yourself a dollar limit for spending on food and drink—and remember to leave enough for the cab fare home.

There are a lot of savings strategies to think about and hopefully you will be able to save a pile of money when you put these in place. And the best bit—none of the strategies has any major impact on your lifestyle. It's all about spending smart.

It can be a long and tedious process to go through all your expenses and implement the saving suggestions. But once you have done it, it is incredibly easy to keep going with it.

CHAPTER NINE

INSURANCES

Greet him with a warm smile and show
sincerity in your desire to please him.
The Good Wife's Guide

*Unless, of course, he works in insurance, in which case apparently
not many people would be happy to see him, let alone desire to
please him. A recent Beaton Consulting and Beyond Blue survey
identified insurance brokers as being in the top 10 professions most
likely to suffer depression—it's not one of those jobs that people are
enthralled to hear about at parties. Still, insurance brokers were only
ranked tenth overall in the survey. Insurance underwriters (the
people who assess the policy applications as opposed to selling the
policies) ranked third.*

*They still both under-rank lawyers, who came in at first place—
apparently around 16 per cent of lawyers who responded to the*

survey had depressive symptoms. Accountants, actuaries, architects and engineers were also included on the list, along with consultants, IT services and patent attorneys. Presumably the remaining professions are a bit more carefree.

Perhaps keep the above survey in mind as you implement this week's financial tip and go easy on your insurance broker (and even easier on the underwriter).

Financial Tip of the Week
Ensure that you insure.

I know it seems a little illogical, telling you to go out and spend money on insurance cover now that we have got your budget and savings in order, but insurance is one of those things that just has to fit into the budget somehow.

There are many types of insurance and ironically, the ones that people usually think of as being the most important, such as car and contents cover, are actually the least important in the scheme of things.

There are two broad types of insurance that we need to look at—general insurance and personal insurance.

GENERAL INSURANCE

We have already covered these insurances in part. General insurances are things such as house, contents and car insurance, as well as health insurance. Insurances that cover things other than your own person. Let's have a look at the main types of cover.

Home and contents insurance

This protects your house and contents from burglary and some natural or accidental mishaps.

It's important to review your home insurance regularly some insurers have an 'underinsurance' clause in their contract which means that if your home is not insured for current prices you may only receive a part payout in the event of something happening. This can be a nasty surprise at the time of the claim.

If you don't own a home it is still a good idea to consider contents insurance. Even if you don't think that you own much you could be surprised at what replacing it would add up to.

Car insurance

When you register your vehicle you also pay Compulsory Third Party (CTP) insurance. This covers injuries to third parties.

You can insure for accidents, broken into or stolen cars and vandalised cars. These sorts of things happen to cars every day. You don't want to run up the backside of someone's Porsche 911—paying for the repairs could end up being your main financial goal for the next 10 years! There are many different levels of insurance and varying premiums, that you can discuss with your insurer of choice.

As I mentioned in Chapter 8, bundling these insurances up into one package with one provider could mean you save money on premiums. Shopping around can save you even more. While there is not usually much difference in the cost of CTP insurance between providers, comprehensive insurance premiums can differ by hundreds of dollars. A survey by Choice <www.choice.com.au> in November 2007 found average annual savings across all states of $2230 for a young driver, $315 for an adult driver and $340 for an older driver, so it certainly pays off to do some research! As always, Choice <www.choice.com.au> is a great reference source, as is the ASIC consumer website <www.fido.gov.au>.

Health insurance

Private health insurance allows you to choose your doctor and hospital and helps you avoid lengthy waiting periods for elective surgery. 'Extras' cover may cover things such as optical, physiotherapy and dental. Everyone has a degree of medical cover through Medicare, private health insurance gives more choice and flexibility—if you want it.

Whether this is high on your priority list is up to you. If you want to go private, do your research on the relevant websites I mentioned in Chapter 8.

Even if private health cover isn't high on your priority list you may want to consider it anyway. The government is keen for as many Australians as possible to hold private cover and they have developed a series of rewards and punishments to encourage us to do so.

The reward is the 30 per cent rebate that the government provides on the cost of the cover. For example, if your health-cover premiums are $2000 per annum the government will rebate to you $600. You can either take this rebate in the form of cheaper premiums or claim it back at tax time.

The punishment is the Lifetime Health Cover provision, which means if you join a health fund after age 30 you will pay a 2 per cent per year surcharge (up to a 70 per cent surcharge). So, if you join a fund at age 40 you will pay 20 per cent more than someone who joined at age 30. Another significant punishment is the Medicare levy surcharge; once your earnings exceed a certain amount (check the Medicare website for current thresholds <www.medicare.gov.au>) you will be charged an extra 1 per cent Medicare levy on your taxable income. At a certain point it is going to become cheaper to just take out insurance!

There are other forms of general insurance such as domestic workers cover and professional indemnity cover, to name a couple. It is beyond the scope of this book to go through every type of cover available and to whom it may apply. A good insurance consultant should be able to take you through the types of cover and the options with regards to each.

PERSONAL INSURANCE

This is insurance that covers you for your life and your death.

People can fall into the trap of not having enough insurance cover. They think that having life insurance to just cover their mortgage in the event of death is sufficient, however what happens to your children's education or your spouse's income if you as the main breadwinner dies? People also think they are

invincible and that they won't get sick or injured.
Statistics show that 1 in 3 people will be off work for
more than 3 months before the age of 65*. When you
consider this, it is a third of the population that will
not have an income for 3 months, so what will
happen to their rent, mortgage, food electricity and
petrol to name just a few?

—*Louisa Chamberlain, Suncorp financial planner*
(*From the Australian Institute of Health and Welfare 2004*)

With this in mind, let's have a look at the main types of
personal insurance cover you need to think about.

Income protection

In your (probable) situation as a double-income, no-kids
couple, this is possibly the most important insurance that
you require. If you have children then life insurance is
equally important. What is income protection? Income
protection provides a regular income in the event that you
are unable to work due to illness or injury. You can
generally insure 75 per cent of your income, including
commissions, and you can choose a waiting period (how
long you have to be off work before the benefit starts being
paid) and an amount of time that the benefit will be paid
to suit your circumstances and your budget. Ideally, you
should choose a policy that pays you a benefit until you
reach retirement age.

It worries me that people will insure their $30,000
vehicle but will neglect to insure their income, which could
be worth a couple of million dollars over the years.

It can be expensive, but there are some strategies to make it cheaper. Firstly, check with your current superannuation fund to see whether you have any automatic salary continuance cover with them. Some superannuation funds will offer up to two years' worth of income protection (for a cost, of course). This means that you can consider taking an external policy to cover your salary to age 65, with a two-year waiting period. This will make the premiums cheaper.

Recent changes to legislation mean that you can now put an income protection policy within your superannuation fund. This can make it easier on your hip pocket for the time being because the premiums for the insurance are taken out of your superannuation contributions rather than your cash in hand.

If you do pay for your income protection from your cash in hand then these premiums are a tax-deductible expense. You will get a reasonable portion of the cost back as a tax refund.

Life insurance

This is another important insurance, particularly if you have a mortgage or other debts and most particularly if you have children. Life insurance provides a lump sum payment to your beneficiaries upon your death. It will help your dependants pay out any debts that you may have together and, if you do have children, provide for future needs such as their education, as well as a lump sum that your partner can invest and gain an income from.

There are numerous ways to work out how much life insurance you should have and to an extent it will depend on whether you have children or not. If not, it is a reasonably simple calculation.

1. Work out what amount would be needed to pay all your debts (for example, mortgage, credit cards, personal loans, investment loans).
2. Work out what funds you already have available (superannuation, current investments and current life insurance).
3. Calculate the difference between the two. This is how much extra life insurance you need.

See Appendix 5 on page 218 for a template to help you do this calculation. If you do have children the calculation has a few more steps.

1. Work out what amount would be needed to pay all your debts (for example, mortgage, credit cards, personal loans, investment loans).
2. Work out the lump sum needed for your children's education and outside school care (for example, they may require a nanny for a few years while they are very young).
3. Work out what income your partner would need to survive on (given that all debts are paid out) over and above their regular income. So, for example, if your partner would continue to earn, say, $40,000 per year after tax, but the expenses would be $50,000 per year,

there would be a $10,000 per year shortfall. You should allow for a lump sum of money that, if invested at 5 per cent after tax, would provide this income. So in this example needing $10,000 per annum you would need a lump sum of around $200,000.
4. Total the three amounts above.
5. Work out what funds you already have available (for example, superannuation, current investments, current life insurance).
6. Calculate the difference between the two. This is how much extra life insurance you need.

Again, see Appendix 5 on page 218 for a template to help you do this calculation. The reason that it is more complex if you have children is because your partner may need to give up work or cut back their work in order to look after the children. And any drop in income needs to be compensated for. If you are double income, no kids then a sudden death is not as financially traumatic. It's still just as emotionally horrible, but to a certain extent the surviving partner can get on with their financial life more easily as there is nobody else depending on them.

To make it easier to afford it is handy to know that life insurance can often be purchased within a superannuation fund. This way the premiums can be paid for through your regular contributions or through any additional contributions you make. Don't do this without obtaining professional advice from your accountant or financial planner as there can be taxation implications if the benefit is ever paid out.

Total and permanent disability (TPD) insurance

This provides a lump sum payment if you suffer an illness or injury which prevents you from ever working again. It is advisable to have at least enough to cover your debts. If you have income protection then that should cover all your other expenses.

This type of cover is often 'attached' to your life cover and, like life insurance, this can also be purchased through superannuation (get professional advice).

Trauma insurance

This provides a lump sum benefit in the event of you suffering a critical condition. What constitutes a critical condition will be defined by the insurance company. It generally covers things such as heart attack, cancer, stroke and other serious conditions.

Ideally, have at least enough cover to pay out your debts and provide a lump sum for lifestyle changes. From there your income protection can pick up the slack.

Unfortunately, trauma insurance cannot be purchased through a superannuation fund—you will have to pay for it out of your own income. It can be expensive so spend some time investigating the options. It's possible to make premiums cheaper by excluding some conditions if you think the cost outweighs the benefit.

Keep in mind that this is all general information. It is important for you to visit a financial planner or insurance broker and with them work through what the optimal amount of personal insurance is for you and your partner and how this should be structured. If you simply cannot afford the optimal cover then work with the planner/broker to find ways to make the premiums cheaper—for example, by putting some cover through superannuation or by taking a longer waiting period on income protection. A good planner will be able to help you with this—check the Financial Planning Association's website <www.fpa.asn.au> for information and tips on how to select a financial planner.

The goal of personal insurance is not to make a large profit in the event of your partner's death; it is to provide adequate cover for you to get by in the lifestyle you are accustomed to.

Let's work through a quick example to see how it all works.

Tom and Sarah have recently bought a house and moved in together. They are both in their twenties and have no children. Sarah has never thought much about insurance or how much she should have. Given that they now have a mortgage and a commitment to each other she decides it's a good time to review it all. Their financial planner helps them work out how much cover she needs.

Death and Total & Permanent Disability
Immediate needs

Mortgage discharge/home provision	*$250,000*
Other outstanding debts (joint car loan)	*$20,000*
Estate and funeral expenses	*$10,000*
Subtotal A	**$280,000**

Less realisable assets

Life insurance (existing)	*$0*
Superannuation	*$30,000*
Subtotal B	**$30,000**
A − B = Cover required	*$250,000*

Critical illness

Total outstanding debts	*$270,000*
Emergency income	*$20,000*
Medical and rehabilitation costs	*$40,000*
Cover required	**$330,000**

Income protection

75% of monthly gross income	*$4,500*
Less existing monthly income protection benefit	*$0*
Required monthly income protection	**$4,500**
How long could you survive without regular income?	*3 months*
How long should the monthly benefit be paid for?	*Until retirement*

Sarah checks with her superannuation fund provider and finds that the Life and TPD cover can be obtained within her superannuation. This way, the cost of the cover will be met by her normal superannuation contributions and not be an additional out-of-pocket expense.

Her fund will also provide two years of income protection insurance, which means that she can then apply for an external policy that has a two-year waiting period. This will significantly reduce the premiums on this.

The only other cover she requires is trauma cover. This can't be placed within superannuation so they manage to pay this out of their normal budget.

Hopefully, this example will make sense. It is a difficult topic to explain succinctly. I strongly recommend that you make an appointment with a professional to go through it with them in detail as there are many other variables to be taken into account. This is just an overview to help you understand how much insurance you might need.

Of course it is ideal if you can afford the optimum level of every insurance cover, but this may not be financially possible. A professional can go through each type of cover with you step by step to work out how to fit the most important covers into your budget. It's boring, I know, but it can be very important for your future quality of life.

CHAPTER TEN

ESTATE PLANNING

Listen to him. You may have a dozen important
things to tell him, but the moment of his arrival
is not the time. Let him talk first—remember
that his topics of conversation are more
important than yours.
The Good Wife's Guide

*And after all, letting your male partner get all his talking done first
day shouldn't take all that long. For the majority of men I'd hazard
a guess that it would be all of about 30 seconds, or however long it
takes to say: 'Where's the remote control? Do we have any beer?'
After that, communication is just a series of grunts.*

*Perhaps I'm being a little harsh, but it is a well-documented fact
that, on average, women enjoy talking, and talk, a great deal more
than men. According to body language expert Allan Pease, women*

use about 20,000 words per day—men use about 7000. Not even half. No wonder they run out of conversation so soon!

There's no doubt about it, men just don't have the verbal stamina. Women, on the other hand, are frequently advised that they could talk underwater, or in their sleep, or underground. Which sort of leads us into this week's topic.

Financial Tip of the Week
Plan your estate.

What do Abraham Lincoln, Peter Brock and Anna Nicole Smith have in common? Well, apart from the fact that they are all dead, they also all died intestate. That is, without having a valid will.

Estate planning is about making sure that your estate can be distributed according to your wishes in a tax-effective manner. It is also about ensuring the security of your assets in the event of something happening to you. It can be a more complex area than you may think.

If you are young with few assets you may wonder if it is really worth the trouble and expense of going to see a solicitor. In a word (or three): yes, it is. No matter what your personal situation, dying intestate is a nuisance at best and a calamity at worst. And there is far more to estate planning than just writing a will.

'We prefer to call it life planning,' says NSW Public Trustee Peter Whitehead. 'It involves spending time considering your future and how you would look after yourself if your circumstances changed. It may include making a power of attorney, writing or updating your will or setting up trusts and it is essential for every Australian. Failing to prepare for your life can really leave your personal circumstances in a mess.'

So what are the main estate planning considerations?

DOING A WILL

Your will is a legal document that instructs how your assets are to be distributed upon your death. It also covers issues such as nominating a guardian for your children and potentially setting up a trust to provide for your family over the years.

If you die without a will, you die 'intestate'. Dying intestate means that a court-appointed administrator will administer your estate. As that administrator will possibly have no idea as to what your wishes were you have no guarantee that what you hoped would happen, will happen. Much better to write a will!

You can choose to visit your solicitor to set up your will, or potentially use a 'do-it-yourself' will kit. Undoubtably a DIY kit is the cheaper option but, to paraphrase Donald Rumsfeld, sometimes you don't know what you don't know. Using a DIY kit denies you the benefits of professional advice and could ultimately turn out to be a false economy.

Some things that you will need to think about before you see your solicitor are as follows:

- Who do you wish to nominate as your executor? Whoever you choose, you should make sure they are comfortable with this potential role. An executor is responsible for the administration of your estate, which may include selling assets, investing funds, submitting tax returns and dividing the estate among your beneficiaries. Settling an estate can be time consuming and can involve a lot of paperwork; it is not a role to be taken on lightly. If you are leaving everything to each other you might make each other executor of your respective wills and nominate another person as back-up in case you both die together. Whoever is executor can always be directed to seek advice from your solicitor and accountant.

- Who do you wish your beneficiaries to be? Is everything to be left to each other or are there extended family and friends who you wish to leave a portion to? Are there any specific bequests you wish to make (that is, specific items that you wish to leave to specific people)? It is a good idea to limit these to a minimum because if you make a specific bequest but then later sell or otherwise dispose of the item, that part of the will can be void and your beneficiary can be left high and dry.
- If you have children you should nominate a guardian for your children in the event that you both die. Again, this is not a role to be taken lightly and should be discussed with the potential guardian before the nomination.

Most assets that you own can be dealt with in your will. The main exceptions that may affect you are:

- some jointly held assets
- superannuation proceeds
- life insurance policy proceeds
- interest that you have as owner or beneficiary of a trust.

An important thing to remember in regard to a will is that marriage will automatically void a pre-existing will, unless it was set up in anticipation of the marriage. Divorce does not void a will, so if the unfortunate happens and you go your separate ways you may need to revise your will.

NOMINATING A POWER OF ATTORNEY

A power of attorney is a legal document that authorises some other person (which may be your spouse, another relative or a friend) to legally act on your behalf. You can nominate this to be for not only your financial affairs but your personal and health issues as well.

A power of attorney is automatically cancelled if the person authorising them becomes mentally incapable. If you have put in place an *enduring* power of attorney, it can continue to operate.

Choosing whom to nominate as your power of attorney requires careful consideration. 'It often requires particular skills involving onerous legal and financial responsibilities and, of course, assumes a great deal of trust,' explains Peter Whitehead. 'Many people appoint family members or friends without realising the burden it can bring.'

And Peter Whitehead warns against procrastination: 'We've seen cases where people have had loved ones develop a mental illness who then face red-tape, confusion and emotional distress because no one thought of setting up an enduring power of attorney,' he says.

A power of attorney can be invaluable in keeping a business ticking along, or even simply keeping your investments running smoothly. Serious illness can cause enough lifestyle problems without being worried about financial problems as well.

SUPERANNUATION

Superannuation deserves a special mention because for many people it can be the largest cash component of their estate. However, as it is not automatically included within your will it is an area that needs special attention.

Have you nominated a beneficiary on your super-annuation fund? It is something that many of us forget to do and this can cause delay, administrative hassle and stress for our surviving relatives.

For most superannuation funds, the payout decision is at the sole discretion of the trustees of the super fund. However, many funds now offer a 'binding death benefit nomination', which allows the member to give a legally binding instruction as to who the money should be paid to. They are a bit of a nuisance from an administrative point of view as they need to be updated regularly (which you will need to remember to do) to remain valid and they will also need to be updated if your personal circumstances change.

There are a number of other more specialised areas of estate planning that are outside the scope of this general overview. Your solicitor can guide you through the complexities of all these areas and help you to set up the best estate plan for your individual situation. Make a written list of questions before your appointment, that way you won't forget anything.

None of us likes to think about dying, but a little bit of preparation could save a lot of delay and confusion.

CHAPTER ELEVEN

CHECK YOUR FIGURES

Make the evening his. Try to understand his
world of strain and pressure and his very real
need to be at home and relaxing.
The Good Wife's Guide

Marriage is an interesting institution. Despite falling church attendance rates and increasing divorce rates, people just keep on doing it (getting married, that is). There is something about it that many of us find compelling—about 100,000 couples per year in Australia take the plunge.

And if you do get married, it certainly seems better from a financial point of view to stay married. In a 2007 research paper[*]

---

[*] 'The consequences of divorce for financial living standards in later life.' David de Vaus, Matthew Gray, Lixia Qu & David Stanton, research paper no. 38, February 2007.

the Australian Institute of Family Studies concluded that older Australians who have been divorced and are still single will on average have lower incomes and fewer assets that their married counterparts.

Not that money alone should be a compelling reason to stay together, so it's good to know that apparently getting married is also good for your health. According to research published in 2006 in the USA Journal of Epidemiology and Community Health, a survey of 80,000 people revealed that those who had never married were 58 per cent more likely to die during the course of the eight-year study than were their married counterparts. It must be that relaxing home atmosphere that makes all the difference!

Financial Tip of the Week
Check on your tracking system.

More an administrative matter than anything, but if you have been working through this book chapter by chapter and implementing the recommendations as you go along then your tracking spreadsheet (remember the tracking system we set up in Chapter 5?) has probably been running for a little over a month by now. If so, it's time to do a reality check and make sure that it is running as it is supposed to.

Grab your current bank statements and open up your computer file or pull out your journal. You need to start ticking them off.

In the same way as when you set up your budget in the first place, the object is to make sure that the figures entered in your tracking spreadsheet match the deposits and withdrawals from your various bank accounts. If you have been entering the figures every day or two there shouldn't be any major discrepancies (beyond perhaps the occasional direct debit or credit that you may have overlooked).

Doing this exercise will enable you to ensure that your spending is on track. In order to compare your overall figures against your overall yearly budget you need to do some 'seasonal adjustments', as economists like to call it.

To do this you need to subtract out eleven-twelfths of any annual expenses that *have* fallen due in this month and add in one-twelfth of any annual expenses that *haven't* fallen due. Likewise, you need to subtract out two-thirds of any quarterly expenses that fell due in this month and add in one-third of any quarterly expenses that *didn't* fall due (I am assuming here that you are using one month of expenses).

Hopefully that paragraph makes sense. The aim is to add in and subtract out the various proportions of expenses that should and shouldn't fall due in that month. For example, if last month you paid your annual motor vehicle insurance of $1200, then leaving this $1200 in your tracking spreadsheet will distort the true amount of your overall expenses on an ongoing basis. So, subtract out eleven-twelfths of the expense. ($1200 divided by 12 = $100. $100 multiplied by 11 = $1100. $1100 should be subtracted from the expense, leaving $100 as the monthly amount in your budget.) Likewise, if this motor vehicle insurance *wasn't* paid last month then you need to add $100 into your monthly tracking figures to give a true reflection of how you are performing against your monthly budget allowance.

This adding in and subtracting out of bits and pieces isn't something that you need to do on a regular basis, it is something to do occasionally to make sure that you are on track and not heading for a big financial fall. After all, money sitting in your bank account can lull you into a false sense of security if you are oblivious to the fact that you have a large expense looming on the horizon.

How do your figures look this month? Are there any nice surprises or nasty shocks? Hopefully you are implementing some of the budgeting savings that we identified in Chapter 8, as well as any others that you came up with, and can start to see these savings reflected in your tracking spreadsheet.

Remember to include the money going into your regular savings plan in your tracking spreadsheet. It is nice to see a figure in there that is doing good, not evil. Hopefully your discretionary and other expenditure has been reduced sufficiently to take account of these savings without putting you into deficit.

I won't keep on reminding you about your tracking spreadsheet, but I do encourage you to keep it going. It can be tedious, yes, but well and truly worth doing for the certainty that it gives you about exactly where your money is going. It is a bit like cleaning your teeth—a frequent task that is not in any way interesting but it provides significant long-term health benefits.

CHAPTER TWELVE

INVESTING

Try to make sure your home is a place of peace, order and tranquillity, where your husband can renew himself in body and spirit.
The Good Wife's Guide

Of course, whether or not your home is a place of peace, order and tranquillity may depend upon what star sign you are and what star sign your partner is and how you react together. Apparently there is such a thing as a 'good cosmic match'.

Personally, I'm not that into star signs. I read my daily horoscope but can't say that I've ever noticed that it's been particularly right. Unless it says something along the lines of 'You will become irrationally annoyed for a period of time today' because that's basically a daily thing for me or 'the idea of overseas travel will be alluring', well, duh! Any of the other eleven horoscopes could be just as applicable.

Still, certain star signs are supposed to attract and more importantly be a good long-term proposition. Although it's never as simple as Aries plus Leo equals Yes, Cancer plus Aquarius equals No.

Astrology may well be a valid study of celestial phenomena and earth events, but I'm just not sure that bedroom events should fall into that category. According to our star signs my husband and I should have separated years ago!

Financial Tip of the Week
Understand investing.

Irrespective of your star sign and whether you turn out to be a rampant materialist or a vividly idealistic socialist, you are going to need some amount of money (and investments) to get by on.

If you have worked your way through each of the previous chapters then you have completed the building blocks of financial management. That is, all those things that you need to get set up and running smoothly before you can think about building your wealth. If you can't manage the money that you have then it's unlikely you will be able to make a great deal more.

But when you can manage what you have, then it's time to look at some big-picture stuff.

Investments. The word may conjure up images of bland, grey-suited finance nerds with glasses and tie-pins rabbiting on about world economic trends and recent fiscal development. Alternatively, you may have mental pictures of super-sleek salesmen verbally caressing you with assurances that, yes, it is possible to be overnight millionaires with the click of a computer key.

Investment reality is far more middle-of-the-road. A good understanding of investment classes or types and how they work will put you ahead of the pack and hold you in good stead throughout your life. There is a mind-boggling plethora of investments in the marketplace, all ready and willing to absorb your money. How on earth do you distinguish between the good, the bad and the ugly, let alone work out what is the right sort of investment for you? Let's start by defining what the main investment types are.

There are basically four main types of investments:

- cash
- fixed interest
- property
- shares.

It may seem hard to believe but all the various products on the market fit into one or more of these categories. Let's look at their main characteristics.

CASH

We all know what cash is, right? Well, maybe. Think about it in these terms: the Australian Securities and Investment Commission (ASIC) website defines cash as 'lending your money in return for payment of interest'. It is worth repeating: you are *'lending your money in return for payment of interest'*. Many people don't consider themselves to be lenders; they simply see themselves as depositing money in an account and being paid a rate of return on that money. It is important to realise that you are acting in the capacity of a lender and charging the borrower an interest rate. It is exactly the same as the bank lending you money for your house or car or any other spending, and it can involve the same risks.

Of course, some cash investments are risk free and some are far less risky than others. A quick rule of thumb for estimating how risky a cash investment might be is the rate of return (interest rate) that is being offered, where the basic cliché usually holds true—that the higher the offered return, the higher the risk. Look at it this way: if a major bank is willing to pay 6 per cent interest to borrow your funds, but another institution is willing to pay 10 per cent to borrow your funds, logic would dictate that the other institution is going to use those borrowed funds in a way that involves greater investment risk for them and hence greater investment risk for you, or that the institution themselves constitutes a greater risk.

A cash investment is an interest-paying investment, which does not provide capital growth. Outlined below are some of the main types of cash accounts available:

- **At call cash account.** These are pretty straightforward. You lend your money to an institution with the option of taking back part or all of the loan at any point in time with no advance notice. The institution pays you interest on the money you have lent to them.

- **Cash management trusts (CMT).** These may be at-call or have a specified time delay between requesting withdrawal and paying back the funds. However, they do not have a term deposit-style maturity date. The institution offering the CMT will provide you with a product disclosure statement.

- **Mortgage offset accounts.** While these are not traditionally included in a list of investments, they are a form of safe and tax-effective investment. If you have a home mortgage your financial institution may set up an 'offset account' held against this mortgage. Basically, what this means is that any money you have sitting in your offset account is deemed to reduce your outstanding loan balance. Each month the bank charges you interest based on your loan balance, so if the deemed balance is lower then less interest is charged that month. Every loan repayment you make is a portion of interest and a portion of capital repayment. If the interest charge is lower then your regular monthly repayment is paying off more capital than it otherwise would.

It is worth looking at an example of this as it is difficult to explain. Suppose you have a current mortgage of $200,000 at 7.5 per cent interest on a 20-year term. If you had an additional $15,000 to pay into an offset account the difference it would make would be as follows:

Loan	Less offset $	Total owing	Interest %	Monthly minimum
$200,000		$200,000	7.50%	$1,613
$200,000	$15,000	$185,000	7.50%	$1,492
Difference				$121

You don't actually receive this difference, as you have to keep your mortgage repayments the same. This means that because you are paying less interest with each monthly mortgage repayment (and paying off more capital), your loan term is reduced. In the above example, if you had the additional $15,000 permanently sitting in an offset account it would reduce your loan term by about three years.

FIXED INTEREST

This is a very similar type of investment to cash as it also pays a return via interest and does not involve capital growth. The main difference is that the funds tend to be invested for a set time frame or for a longer term.

- **Government bonds.** This involves lending your money to the government for a set period of time at a set interest rate. As the principal and interest are government guaranteed, this is a highly secure form of cash lending. Interest rates tend to be lower because of this security.
- **Term deposits.** Another straightforward one. You lend your money to a bank or other prudentially regulated group for a set period of time at a set interest rate.

Term deposits are low risk because the institutions offering them are regulated by the Australian Prudential Regulations Authority (APRA). This will be reflected in interest rates.

- **Debentures and unsecured notes.** These are offered to investors through a prospectus and are issued by a company wishing to raise money. As always, remember that the higher the return, the higher the risk. I would recommend that you refer to the education available on ASIC's consumer website <www.fido.gov.au> to thoroughly familiarise yourself with the characteristics of these types of investments before deciding to invest.
- **Mortgage trusts.** Also offered via a prospectus. Although they sound more like a property investment, mortgage trusts are also a form of cash lending. Basically, a mortgage trust takes your money, and the money of other investors, and lends it to other parties for investment in property. You will receive a rate of return based on the interest that those other parties are paying for your money. Some mortgage trusts are registered, which means that they hold an ASIC licence and are regulated by ASIC. However, some schemes are unregistered and are not regulated at all. Do your homework.

PROPERTY

Just as there are numerous cash investments available, there are also numerous property investments available. The return that you receive on property investment will usually be a portion of interest (in the form of rental return) and a portion of capital growth (as the value of your property investment grows). You can either invest in property directly or through a managed fund. The main types of property investment are:

- **Your own home.** If you own your own house, don't forget that as well as being the place you live it is also a property investment. Even better, it doesn't attract any capital gains tax upon sale. Real estate agents will often tell you that position is the most important thing to consider when buying. Obviously, whatever you buy has to fit within your budget, but always look at potential purchases objectively.
- **Residential property.** Much the same as your own home, except someone else will be living in it. Residential property includes houses, units, serviced apartments and any other form of housing accommodation that somebody will pay you rent to live in. The return on your money is in the form of rental and potential capital growth.
- **Commercial property.** This is basically property that somebody will pay you rent for in order to run a business from it. This includes industrial, office and retail spaces. Again, the return on your money is in the form of rental (and will usually be a higher percentage of rental return than residential property) and potential capital growth.
- **Property trusts.** These may be listed on the stock exchange or unlisted (private investments). Property

trusts pool the money of a number of investors to purchase mainly commercial property, which can be very handy if you do not have enough money to purchase property by yourself. Upon investment you will be allocated a certain number of 'units' in the trust, which can be sold to other trust members or the general public. The aim is to receive a rental return plus capital growth. Listed property trusts are probably a better option for inexperienced investors as they can be bought and sold on the stockmarket and hence have a greater level of liquidity.

- **Managed funds**. A managed fund also pools your money with that of other investors. You will be provided with a product disclosure statement prior to purchase and upon purchase will be allocated 'units' in the managed fund, which can be bought or redeemed, usually with little restriction. Managed funds can be a great way of getting into the market, particularly if you do not have enough money to purchase a property by yourself. They also generally offer good diversification, in that they invest in a range of properties as opposed to just one. A managed fund can also give you exposure to international investment, which may otherwise be impractical to consider.

- **Timeshare**. Often not really an investment as they tend to be purchased for lifestyle reasons. However, they are a form of managed fund, although generally lack the liquidity of other managed funds (they may be hard to sell). It's best to look at this as a lifestyle choice rather than an investment.

SHARES

> From an altruistic point of view, companies ultimately
> reflect the endeavours (for better or worse) of the
> human race. From an investment standpoint they are
> the wealth creators making the world go round.
> Everyone, from children to grandparents, can benefit
> from investing in shares.
>
> —*Peter Thornhill, founder of* <www.motivatedmoney.com

When you buy shares you are buying a slice of ownership
in a company. You are effectively making a statement that
you believe this particular company is well managed, has a
solid cash flow and good growth prospects. The return you
receive on share investment will usually be a slice of
company earnings, in the form of dividends, and potential
capital growth over time. Shares can be an extremely
rewarding form of investment, however, as with all
investments it is important to thoroughly do your
homework first. You can either invest in shares directly or
through a managed fund and the main types of investment
are:

- **Australian listed shares.** Most people are familiar
  with many stock exchange listed shares, the names of
  these appear daily—Coles, Woolworths, ANZ, Telstra, to
  name just a few. These are companies in which you can
  buy a slice of ownership. As with any other investment,
  get professional advice before you buy. To my mind the
  biggest mistake that some people make when they
  decide to 'dabble in the sharemarket' is to buy shares

based solely on the advice of family or friends, or because of a red-hot tip they read on the internet or in the newspaper. They eagerly buy a particular share, then watch it decrease in value. They panic, pull their money out and label shares as a 'risky investment'. Anything would be risky based on that type of investment strategy! Stock exchange listed shares are a liquid asset (they can usually be sold easily). The return on listed shares is via dividends and potential capital growth. Some Australian listed shares pay you a 'franked dividend', which can be a great tax advantage. We will cover this in Chapter 14.

- **Unlisted shares.** You may have the opportunity to buy shares in an unlisted Australian company. Most often this may be the company that you work for. The basic principle is the same as for listed shares—you are purchasing a slice of ownership in the company. It is harder to obtain professional advice on the value of the investment, although your accountant may be able to provide you with a cost/value formula to use. You may view purchasing shares as a sign of commitment to the business, or as a way of gaining management influence. It is still a good idea to assess the purchase as you would any other investment, namely, what is the quality of the management team, what are the dividend prospects and what the long-term growth prospects of the business are.

- **International listed shares.** In the same way as you can buy shares listed on the Australian sharemarket you can also purchase shares listed on international markets.

This can give you exposure to some of the largest companies in the world. Again, the expected return would be via dividends and capital growth. However, an additional factor that you need to consider when investing overseas is currency fluctuations. A rising Australian dollar can reduce the value of your overseas-held investments and likewise a falling Australian dollar can increase the value. This is separate to the rise or fall based on business performance.

- **Managed funds.** Like property-based managed funds, share-based managed funds pool your money with that of other investors. You will be provided with a product disclosure statement prior to purchase and upon purchase will be allocated 'units' in the managed fund, which can be bought or redeemed, usually with little restriction. Managed funds, in my view, are an excellent way of owning shares as not only are you benefiting from the professional experience of a fund manager, you are gaining a far greater diversification across shares and industries and even countries than you could by investing directly.

What a long list. And these are just the main types of general investments. There are all sorts of other investment terms floating around, such as exchange traded options, stapled securities, hedge funds, futures, agricultural schemes, warrants, to name a few. But always keep in mind that, no matter what type of investment is being marketed, it is still investing in either cash, fixed interest, property or shares (or a combination of these things).

Sometimes sales and marketing campaigns can be very slick and impressive. Always, *always* do your research through a professional organisation before parting with your hard-earned cash. And always remember that if something sounds too good to be true, it probably is.

CHAPTER THIRTEEN

TAXING ISSUES

Don't greet him with complaints or problems.
The Good Wife's Guide

It's always nice to start off on the right foot, isn't it? The way that you greet each other can set the tone for the rest of the evening, and we all like to have a good evening.

To help my readers have a good evening, I conducted a pop quiz of males and females to find out what an ideal greeting from their partner might be.

Women greeting their partner could say:

- *How was your day? Let me get you a beer.*
- *Yes, this is Victoria's Secret lingerie. Do you like it?*
- *Sit down, let me give you a shoulder massage.*
- *I was just about to strip off and have a shower. Want to join me?*

Men greeting their partner could say:

- *Sit and relax. I'll cook dinner—and clean up afterwards.*
- *You look fantastic in that new outfit/with that new hairstyle.*
- *Sit down, let me give you a shoulder massage.*
- *I was just about to strip off and have a shower—do you want me to put the rubbish bins out first?*

Financial Tip of the Week
Don't pay more tax than you need to.

Of course no matter how warm your greetings are, there is one person that it's hard to be enthusiastic about—the tax commissioner, poor chap.

Around 11.5 million Australians lodge a tax return each year and we claim around $27 billion in total deductions, about half of which is for work-related expenses.

> Work-related expenses present a continuing
> compliance challenge for us. We review claims that are
> outside normal patterns and the claims of people
> identified as being at risk of not complying.
> —*Michael D'Ascenzo, Tax Commissioner*

It's always a flurry at the end of the financial year (it is for me, anyway) to find all our paperwork and get it into some sort of order, ready for the accountant. Whether you are a DIY online tax return person or whether you hand it all over to a tax agent there is a certain amount of paperwork and headache involved. So while it is vital to heed the commissioner's instruction not to overstate your expenses, it's also important to ensure that all the tax-time hassle is made worthwhile by not understating your expenses.

How do you ensure that you are making the most of our taxation legislation? First and foremost it helps if you understand how our Australian tax system works. We pay tax on a progressive scale (as opposed to a flat rate). Current income tax rates applicable from the 2008/2009 year, as at time of writing are as follows:

Taxable income	Tax on this income
$0 – $6,000	0.00%
$6,001 – $34,000	15c for each dollar over $6,000
$34,001 – $80,000	$4,200 + 30c for each dollar over $34,000
$80,001 – $180,000	$18,100 + 40c for each dollar over $80,000
$180,001 and above	$58,100 + 45c for each dollar over $180,000

Plus Medicare levy of 1.5%

For up-to-date income tax rates check out the Australian Taxation Office (ATO) website <www.ato.gov.au>—my favourite bedtime reading (just kidding).

Your top tax rate is known as your marginal tax rate. This is the percentage of tax that you pay on the top margin of your income. For example, if you earn $85,000 then your marginal tax rate would be 40 per cent — that is, 40 cents in each dollar you earn above $80,000.

Most adults have to pay tax, it's a fact of life but nobody in their right mind wants to pay more tax than they need to. It makes sense to spend some time making sure that you (a) claim a deduction for everything that you are entitled to claim, and (b) structure your investments as tax effectively as possible.

MAXIMISING YOUR DEDUCTIONS

- **First and foremost—*keep accurate records*.** This is the most simple thing in the world to do. Just get a manila folder and write 'TAX 2008/2009' (or whatever year it is for) at the top. Keep the folder stored somewhere accessible and file all your receipts and income statements in it each week. If you are not sure if something is a deduction toss it in the folder anyway and check it out at a later date. All you have to do at the end of financial year is pull out the folder and put the paperwork in order. No searching through the house, car, office drawers and handbag for scraps of (probably unidentifiable) paper.
- **Keep all medical receipts as well.** You are able to claim a 20 per cent rebate on out-of-pocket medical expenses over a certain limit. The expenses of both of you (if you are married or considered de facto) can be added together to reach this limit. A tip is to allocate one of you to pay all medical expenses during the year.
- **Keep your records for at least five years.** At the time you submit your tax return the ATO takes your

word for the honesty of your estimates, but they have up to five years to come back to you and request an audit. If you cannot substantiate your claim you will be penalised. Store your records somewhere safe.

- **Claim all your work-related expenses**. Work-related expenses are those that you incur as an employee while performing your job. It depends on the type of work you do as to what may be claimable by you. There are generic items such as union fees, trade magazines or books and work-related seminars that are applicable to anyone. Other items will be dependent on your type of work. The ATO website provides a list of commonly claimable items, as well as tax rulings for specific professions ranging from airline employees to performing artists. Check these out at <www.ato.gov.au>. Alternatively, if you are still unsure about a particular item telephone the ATO—they are a very helpful bunch.
- A few work-related expenses deserving of special mention are: **income protection insurance**—the premium that you pay for this is a tax deduction. As are **self-education expenses**, provided the education is related to your income earning activity. Computer costs, for a work-related computer, if borne by you are deductible, as is a **laptop bag**. A **briefcase** and an **electronic diary** may be deductible if required for your work. If you use your car for work then **car expenses** may be deductible (this does not include travelling to and from work). Another deduction is **work-related phone calls**.

- **Claim the cost of doing your tax**. Accountant's and tax agent's fees are tax deductible, as are the cost of telephone calls and faxes to them and travel to see them.
- **Donations to charities are a tax deduction**.
- You may be able to claim a **dependant spouse offset**. See the ATO website for details.
- The **interest cost of investment loans** will be a tax deduction where those investments are earning an income for you. On the flipside, don't forget to add the income earned from your investments into your tax return.
- **Depreciation** may be claimable on investment buildings and their fittings.
- The **ongoing fees** that you pay to your financial planner (and I do recommend that everyone has one) are a tax deduction.
- If you work from home you may be able to claim **home office expenses**. This is a tricky area to summarise in a few words, so I recommend you look on the ATO website and speak with your accountant.
- **Don't forget dividend imputation**. It is such a wonderful thing! If you own Australian shares, either directly or through a managed fund, the dividends that you receive each year may be 'franked'. This means that the company paying the dividend has already paid tax on the money, of up to 30 per cent (fully franked) or a lesser amount (partially franked). This tax that the company has already paid will be a tax rebate for you, called a 'franking credit'. It makes some Australian

shares and managed funds a very tax effective form of investment.

This is not an exhaustive list of tax deductions and offsets, just some of the more common ones. As I mentioned, check the ATO website for tax rulings regarding your profession or give them a call.

QUICK TAX DEDUCTION HITS

You may be getting close to the end of financial year and starting to get a sinking feeling that you are going to end up with a tax bill this year (that is, a demand to pay even *more* tax). This can happen for several reasons: perhaps your investments did particularly well income-wise, or perhaps you received some income from a source other than your employer that wasn't subject to PAYG (pay as you go) tax. For whatever reason you need an immediate tax-deduction hit—fast!

- **Pre-pay some expenses**. If you require a quick tax deduction hit then consider pre-paying some work-related expenses. If your cash flow allows you can consider pre-paying some of your deductible expenses, such as income protection or interest on an investment loan.
- **Salary sacrifice** into superannuation. Again, if your cash flow allows (and your payroll department is willing) you could consider salary sacrificing some of your earnings between now and the end of tax year

into your superannuation fund. Keep in mind that this does lock the money away until your future retirement.

- **Offset capital gains with capital losses.** If you have incurred capital gains through sale of any investments over the tax year, these can be offset against capital losses. So perhaps review the investments you hold and consider whether it could be worth selling any poorly performing items.

STRUCTURE INVESTMENTS TAX-EFFECTIVELY

- **Don't hold cash investments when you have personal debts**. Unless, of course, the cash funds are being held for a specific short-term purpose. Otherwise it makes no sense to hold a cash account earning maybe 6 per cent *before tax*, when you could potentially use a mortgage offset account, where your money will effectively 'earn' the mortgage interest rate tax free.

- **Investments that are not negatively geared.** (This means you haven't borrowed money to invest in them and they are not making a loss.) These should generally be held in the name of the *lowest income earner*. This is because earnings on these investments will be taxed at the owner's marginal tax rate (MTR). If your MTR is 40 per cent and your partner's MTR is 30 per cent, they will pay 10 per cent less tax on the earnings. For example, say your managed fund has income earnings of $2000. At a MTR of 40 per cent you will lose $800 of these earnings in tax; at a MTR of 30 per cent you would only lose $600 of the earnings in tax.

- **Investments that are negatively geared should usually be owned by the higher income earner**. It is the above example in reverse. If your negatively geared investment makes a loss of $2000, this will result in a tax deduction to someone on a 40 per cent MTR of $800 and a tax deduction to someone on a 30 per cent MTR of $600. Of course this does not take into account potential capital gains tax down the track when the investment is eventually sold. My argument is that there are ways to reduce a person's marginal tax rate in a particular year if required (through use of deductions etc.) and it is better to have the certainty of greater tax deductions now. This is something to discuss in detail with your accountant.

- **Make donations in the name of the highest income earner**. Again, because the dollar amount of tax deduction will be higher.

- For god's sake *don't get sucked into 'tax-effective' schemes*. Towards the end of the financial year there is usually an influx of marketing to consumers about various tax-effective investments. Always look beyond the promised tax deduction to the quality of the underlying investment. No point wasting $1000 on a dud investment just to get a $400 tax refund. The Australian Securities and Investments Commission website <www.fido.gov.au> has some very good information on this subject with tips and traps for unwary players.

All the above information is an overview and not a comprehensive list of deductions and strategies. Hopefully, it will point you in the right direction to start your own search.

Some people do their own tax to save the maybe $200 it would cost to use a tax agent or accountant. Many more people only phone their accountant after the end of the financial year when they are ready to hand over their paperwork. In my opinion these are both false economies. Use a professional and use them properly.

First, outsource your tax to a professional as it will save you time, stress and (because you are handing your tax over to someone who makes it their full-time job to *do* tax), probably money. Second, make the most of their expertise. Go to see them a month or so *before* the end of the financial year and give them a brief rundown of your likely earnings and expenses this year. Ask them for their professional advice—is there anything you should be doing over the next couple of months to reduce your tax? Again, I'm not talking about dodgy tax-effective schemes, I'm talking about effective, worthwhile strategies such as salary sacrifice or pre-payment. It is too late to mention this after the end of the financial year as your records have been finalised by then.

At the end of the day, the ATO doesn't care if you pay them too much—that's your prerogative. But I, for one, can certainly think of *much* better things to do with my money.

CHAPTER FOURTEEN

BORROWING FOR INVESTMENT

Arrange his pillow and offer to take off his shoes.
Speak in a low, soothing and pleasant voice.
The Good Wife's Guide

One of my colleagues snorted that if she was to remove her partner's shoes at the end of a long working day, before he had had a chance to have a shower, then the gas mask she would need to wear would make a low and soothing voice impossible. Obviously our foremothers were made of sterner stuff!

And the whole smell thing is interesting because it is an (apparently) scientifically proven fact that we sniff out our ideal mates. A bit like dogs.

A recent study published in Psychological Science *suggested that women are attracted to men who have different genetic characteristics from them and that they can detect these differences by smell. (The researchers tested this by having women sniff a selection of dirty T-shirts and picking out the smells they liked best—yuck!)*

Unfortunately, the researchers also found that being on the contraceptive pill impaired the women's sense of smell and made them more likely to choose the opposite T-shirts than the ones they would have chosen if they weren't on the pill (if that sentence makes sense). This has potentially serious implications for a long-term relationship. What if you were on the pill when you met your partner and found him wildly sexy, but then a year or so down the track went off the pill and found that he was pretty damn average? Hmmm.

Financial Tip of the Week
Learn about borrowing to invest.

I am sure that you will be relieved to know that my (above) rambling has nothing whatsoever to do with this week's topic. Once you have your day-to-day finances under control and have protected your future wealth via insurance and estate planning and all the other things that we have done so far, something that you can consider as a wealth-building tool is borrowing to invest, or 'gearing' as it is known.

First things first. When you invest in something (other than cash), the return that you receive on your money is divided into two types—income and capital growth. **Income** is the regular inflow of money that you receive from the investment—in the case of property it is usually rental return, in the case of shares it is usually dividends. **Capital growth** is the increase in the value of your investment over time. For example, the increase in the value of your rental property or the increase in value of your shares. This is a return that you don't receive until you sell the investment. Both of these types of return are taxed (the government rarely likes to miss out on anyone else's good fortune). On the income you receive you will pay income tax each year as part of your tax return; on the capital growth you will pay capital gains tax in the financial year in which you sell the asset, also as part of your tax return. You need to understand the whole income and capital growth concept in order to make sense of gearing.

So what is gearing? It's when you borrow money to buy an investment. There are three types of gearing. Your investment could be:

- **Positively geared**—this means that you are earning more in income than you pay out in costs.
- **Neutrally geared**—where you earn roughly the same amount in income as you pay out in costs.
- **Negatively geared**—where the cost of holding the investment is greater than the income you earn from owning it.

Looking at those definitions you may be wondering who in their right mind would borrow money to invest in something that costs them more to own than they earn from it in income. Basically, when you negatively gear into an investment you are wagering that your regular annual losses from holding the investment are going to be more than outweighed by the eventual capital gain that you hope to make when you sell the investment. This can be a valid investment strategy.

When you negatively gear into an investment you are probably also calculating on the investment becoming neutrally geared and then positively geared over a period of time, through increased rental income or dividend income.

The strategy is not without its risks, though. Borrowing to invest magnifies your profits and also magnifies your losses.

What does this mean?

Let's say that you have $100,000 to invest in shares. You are trying to decide whether to simply invest your own $100,000, or whether to invest this $100,000 *plus* borrow an extra $100,000 as well. Let's look at how that decision would affect your profit if the sharemarket rose by 20 per cent.

Your money	$100,000	Your money	$100,000
Borrowed funds	$100,000		
Total investment	$200,000		$100,000
Market rises by	20%		20%
'Profit'	$40,000		$20,000

Looks good, doesn't it? By borrowing money to invest, you have doubled your gain. If you cashed out the investment and repaid the loan, you would have $140,000 in your pocket—that's a 40 per cent gain on your own funds. Hooray!

But what if the market goes down? It's not such a pretty result.

Your money	$100,000	Your money	$100,000
Borrowed funds	$100,000		
Total investment	$200,000		$100,000
Market drops by	20%		20%
'Loss'	$40,000		$20,000

Uh oh, not so good. It's bad enough losing 20 per cent of your own money, but if you are losing 20 per cent of the borrowed money as well, it's a double whammy. In this case, if you cashed out the investment and repaid the loan, you would be left with only $60,000. That's quite a hit!

So gearing is not for everyone and not for every investment. But if you have the cash flow and can access the tax benefits, then borrowing to invest can be a worthwhile way of building your wealth. Let's look at a couple of examples of how gearing might work.

For all the examples assume that the couple, Mick and Sue, each have salary incomes of $50,000 per annum and tax deductible expenses of $4000. They each pay tax of approximately $9090, giving them both a cash flow after costs and tax of $36,910.

Example 1
Positively geared
Mick and Sue have recently purchased a commercial property as an investment. They hope to gain both income and capital growth from this investment. The details of the purchase are as follows:

	$	$
Cost of property (incl. stamp duty and capital expenditure). This amount has been borrowed.	300,000	
Interest rate on borrowings	8.00%	
Annual cost of borrowing	$24,000	
Other annual costs	$6,000	
Total annual cost		$30,000
Monthly rental	$2,800	
Multiplied by 12 months		$33,600

In their tax return, this would be shown as:

Tax return for Mick

Income	$
Salary	50,000
Rental income (Mick's share)	16,800
Total income	66,800
Less expenses	
Work related expenses	4,000
Investment expenses (Mick's share)	15,000
Total expenses	19,000
Taxable income	**47,800**
Approximate tax payable	**9,657**

Cash flow for Mick	$
Total income	66,800
Less total expenses	19,000
Less tax	9,657
Funds available for living expenses	**38,143**

As you can see, Mick's (and Sue's) cash flow has increased to $38,143 each per annum (an increase of $1233 each) as a result of their commercial property investment.

Example 2
Neutrally geared

Mick and Sue have recently purchased a share portfolio as an investment. The details of the purchase were as follows:

	$	$
Cost of share portfolio. This amount has been borrowed.	300,000	
Interest rate on borrowings	8.00%	
Annual cost of borrowing	24,000	
Total annual cost		24,000
Annual dividends – fully franked	16,800	
Plus franking credit	7,200	24,000

(Please note that at the end of this chapter I have given an explanation of 'franking' and how it works on page 143.)

In their tax return, this would be shown as:

Tax return for Mick

Income	$
Salary	50,000
Dividends (Mick's share)	8,400
Plus franking credit	3,600
Total income	62,000
Less expenses	
Work related expenses	4,000

Investment expenses (Mick's share)	12,000
Total expenses	16,000
Taxable income	**46,000**
Approximate tax payable	**9,090**
Less franking credit	**3,600**
Total tax	**5,490**

Cash flow for Mick	**$**
Total income	58,400
Less total expenses	16,000
Less tax	5,490
Funds available for living expenses	**36,910**

In this example, holding the investment would result in exactly the same cash flow for Mick and Sue and it would be neutrally geared.

Example 3
Negatively geared

Mick and Sue have recently purchased a residential property as an investment. The details of the purchase are as follows:

	$	$
Cost of property (inc. stamp duty and capital expenditure). This amount has been borrowed.	300,000	
Interest rate on borrowings	8.00%	
Annual cost of borrowing	$24,000	
Other annual costs	$4,000	

Total annual cost		$28,000
Monthly rental	$1,500	
Multiplied by 12		$18,000

In their tax return, this would be shown as:

Tax return for Mick

Income	$
Salary	50,000
Rental income (Mick's share)	9,000
Total income	59,000
Less expenses	
Work related expenses	4,000
Investment expenses (Mick's share)	14,000
Total expenses	18,000
Taxable income	**41,000**
Approximate tax payable	**7,515**

Cash flow for Mick	$
Total income	59,000
Less total expenses	18,000
Less tax	7,515
Funds available for living expenses	**33,485**

As you can see from the figures above, holding the investment property is going to cost Mick and Sue $3425 each, or around $130 per fortnight out of their own pockets, after taking into account the available tax deductions and so forth. In other words, the investment is negatively geared.

I have used three different types of investments in my examples above; don't take this to mean that commercial property is always positively geared and residential property is always negative and shares always break even—this is not the case. Every time you are considering borrowing money to invest, the merits of the specific investment you are considering need to be weighed up and any out-of-pocket costs of holding the investment need to be considered against predicted capital gain.

Just to complicate things even more, the above examples are based on an investor on a marginal tax rate of 30 per cent. In the previous chapter we looked at current income tax rates. As I mentioned in that chapter, the higher your marginal tax rate, the more tax benefit you will receive from holding negatively geared investments.

What do I mean by this? Well, consider somebody claiming a $10,000 deduction. On a 30 per cent tax rate they could expect to receive $3000 of this cost back as a tax break. On a 45 per cent tax rate they could expect to receive $4500 back as a tax break. But on a 17 per cent tax rate they could only expect to receive $1700 back as a tax break.

Isn't this a fun subject?

Any time that you are considering borrowing money to invest it is wise to get professional advice beforehand. And by 'professional' I don't mean a presenter of a 'get-rich-quick' seminar or a super-smooth salesperson spruiking the benefits of the latest and greatest 'tax effective investment'. I mean your accountant and your financial planner. Preferably both. They can review your intended purchase from a tax and investment perspective and advise you on whether it stacks up in terms of future wealth creation.

How do you know if borrowing to invest is right for you? There is no one perfect answer but I've listed some of the main considerations.

- **What is your investment time frame**? That is, for how long do you want to invest your money? It can take five to 10 years to make a worthwhile sum of money from property or share investment, and will your money be invested for this long? If you know that you want to use your money for something else within a year or two, then property and share investment probably isn't appropriate. Of course, you could be lucky enough to make a good profit in the first year but depending on that type of luck is tempting financial hardship.

- **Would you panic if the market dropped**? Property and sharemarkets can go down as well as up. It's the boom/bust cycle that you hear about. If you are going to invest in these markets then you need to be confident that busts wouldn't keep you awake at night. If you suspect that you might panic and sell at the wrong time, then perhaps these types of investments aren't for you.

- **What is your marginal tax rate**? When you borrow money for an income-producing investment you can claim the cost of borrowings as a tax deduction. The higher your marginal tax rate, the greater the deduction you will receive. You need to ensure that you can claim back enough of the cost of borrowing to make it an attractive proposition.

- **What is the opportunity cost of your money?** By borrowing to invest you are tying up a proportion of both your equity and your cash flow that you could use elsewhere. Consider other options for your money before committing your funds.
- **Check the fundamentals of the investment**. Does it have a good cash flow and a steady rate of capital growth?
- **If the realistic capital growth is not going to compensate you over time for your yearly out-of-pocket expenses, then the investment is not fundamentally good.**

Finally, further to Example 2.

FRANKING CREDITS

When you invest in Australian shares, the income that you receive is in the form of a dividend. Sometimes this dividend, when paid to you, will be described as a 'franked' dividend (it might be either 'fully franked' or 'partially franked'). What this means is that the company has already paid income tax on the money that it is paying out to you.

- 'Unfranked' means that the company has not paid any tax on the dividend that it is paying to you.
- 'Partially franked' means that the company has paid tax on some of the dividend that it is paying out to you.
- 'Fully franked' means that the company has paid tax on all of the dividend that it is paying out to you.

Companies currently pay tax at a flat rate of 30 per cent. When they pay you your dividend you will receive a certain amount of cash, plus a statement detailing your 'franking credit' (the amount of tax the company has already paid on this money).

The ATO, in it's typically good-hearted way, wants to make sure that you do not pay tax on this money twice, so it asks you to pay tax on the full amount of dividend but then gives you a rebate for the tax already paid by the company. In order to do this the ATO asks you to 'add back' the amount of franking credit that you have received. It then taxes you on the full amount and provides you with a rebate for the tax already paid.

As an example, assume that you have received a 'fully franked' cash dividend of $7000. The company has already paid tax at 30% per cent and has also given you a statement showing a 'franking credit' of $3000. This would go in your tax return as follows.

	$
Income	
Salary	60,000
Dividend	7,000
Franking credit	3,000
Total income	**70,000**
Less tax	16,350
Medicare levy	1,050
Total tax	**17,400**
Less franking credit	3,000
Total tax payable	**14,400**

You add the franking credit back into your taxable income, even though it is not cash that you have received. You then subtract out the franking credit from your tax payable at the end of the procedure.

CHAPTER FIFTEEN

SUPERANNUATION

Don't ask him questions about his actions or
question his judgement or integrity.
The Good Wife's Guide

I reckon the above quote manifests itself most obviously when men are driving somewhere and are lost. Of course, they're not really lost, are they? Because men never get lost when driving. The majority of men would rather to do an extra hour's worth of driving than consult a street directory. And they would rather drive across two states than pull over and ask a stranger for directions. And as for changing lanes or doing a U-turn to pull into a service station—well, I don't think it's ever happened.

Take this car conversation:

'*Tom, are we on the right road? I don't recognise this area.*'

'Of course we're on the right road, Jane. It's just a short cut, that's all.'

'Well, we really should have been there by now, it's not much of a short cut.'

'Don't be stupid, woman.'

Half an hour later...

'Are you really sure you know where we are, Tom? We've been driving quite a while.'

'Of course I know. Don't nag.'

'Maybe we could pull over and have a look at the map?'

'We don't have a map. I don't need a map.'

'Look, there's a service station coming up on the right-hand side. Let's just pull over and ask someone.'

'Don't be silly, the servo's on the other side of the road. We'll keep going.'

Half an hour later...

'I swear to God, Tom, if you don't stop and ask someone where we are I'm going to kill you.'

'For God's sake stop nagging.'

*'You ******* **** STOP THIS CAR!'*

Financial Tip of the Week
Make the most of your superannuation.

How many superannuation funds do you have?

Another thing that people, both males and females, aren't particularly good at asking about is their superannuation. As a financial planner it's something that I've seen time and time again—couples with fantastic planning in terms of budgeting and saving and tracking, but they have no idea where their superannuation is or what it's doing.

Superannuation is one of those 'out of sight, out of mind' things. An asset that many of us have but many of us tend to forget about. Nevertheless, it could be one of your most significant assets by the time you retire in the (probably quite distant) future, so it does make sense to review it now and then, making sure you are getting the most from it.

Did you know, for example, that an extra $10,000 paid into your super fund now could, earning 8 per cent per annum, give you an extra $31,000 lump sum at your retirement in around 30 years? Or that if you earn less than $28,000 and put $1000 into your super fund, the government may put in an extra $1500? Or even that an extra 2 per cent of extra return on your $60,000 fund could make a $100,000 difference to your retirement benefit in 30 years?

First things first—there are a few questions you need to ask yourself with regards to your superannuation:

- Are you making the most of what you have?
- Are you taking advantage of all the features?
- Should you be putting more money into it?

MAKING THE MOST OF WHAT YOU HAVE

Forget about contributing extra money, let's concentrate on maximising the value of what you have. There are lots of ways to do this.

- **Consolidate all your superannuation funds.**
  If you have had more than one job or one employer
  since you left school, chances are you have more than
  one superannuation fund. Many of us are very slack
  about remembering to keep them all together or even
  to keep track of them over time. Eventually we run the
  risk of forgetting about them and losing them
  altogether. Did you know that the Australian
  government currently has around $9.7 *billion* of
  unclaimed superannuation sitting in its coffers? Not
  only will consolidating your funds stop you from losing
  track of your money, it will prevent you paying more
  than one set of administration fees. Consolidating
  superannuation funds is easy—the fund that you
  currently use can give you transfer forms to complete
  and send back to them and they will take care of the
  rest.
- **Track down lost superannuation.** If you think you
  may have superannuation sitting around somewhere
  that you have lost track of, then do a search of the Lost
  Member's Register. This is a central register, maintained
  by the Australian Tax Office, to which all
  superannuation providers report. You can request your
  current fund to do this for you or you can do it
  yourself via the ATO website (type 'superseeker' into
  the search box). If this doesn't help you, then make a
  list of your previous employers (and roughly the time
  frame you worked for them) and give them all a call.
  Ask them whether you had superannuation and if so
  where it was paid to. You can then give the relevant

super fund a call and track it down that way. Be mindful of any name changes you have had, address changes and also be aware of the fact that they may not have had your tax file number recorded.

- **Consider the investment option your money is in.** Most superannuation funds offer a wide range of investment options (that is, the different types of investments your money is placed in). In Chapter 12 we looked at the main types of investments and their characteristics. Your superannuation money may be sitting in anything from a cash fund, to balanced growth, shares, property or internally geared, with many others in between. Deciding what type of investment to invest your superannuation into is really something that you need to discuss with a financial planner. As a rule of thumb, the longer your investment time frame (and remember, superannuation will be there until you retire after age 60), the more growth assets you should consider (property and shares). Having your superannuation sitting in a cash-based account earning 4 per cent for 30 years will result in a significantly smaller end balance than the same money sitting in a share-based account earning 8 per cent for 30 years. Talk this over with a financial planner.
- **Should you consider switching funds?** In 2005 the Australian government introduced choice of fund legislation, to give most Australian workers more flexibility about where their superannuation is invested. You will need to check with your employer whether you do have this flexibility. If so, it may be worthwhile

doing some homework about the fees and long-term performance of your current fund compared to the fees and long-term performance of other funds. This can be a tedious task, but the Investment and Financial Services Association (IFSA) has tried to simplify it by comparing a number of the better-known funds. Check their website <www.ifsa.com.au>

TAKING ADVANTAGE OF THE FEATURES

- **List a beneficiary.** A beneficiary is the person who you want your money to be paid to in the event of your death. Superannuation does not form part of your estate (it won't be dealt with through your will). This is mentioned in Chapter 10 and is worth going over again. Your super may be one of your major assets by the time you die and it's important to ensure that you have a beneficiary listed to make it easier for the trustees of the super fund to pay the money out as soon as possible.
- **Consider placing personal insurance cover through superannuation.** I mentioned in Chapter 9 the fact that life, total and permanent disability (TPD) and income protection insurance can often be placed within your superannuation fund. Doing this means that you don't have the expense of these insurance premiums coming out of your bank account. The premiums will be deducted from the balance of your superannuation fund. Either way you are still paying for it, but it can be a useful strategy if your cash flow is

tight. Alternatively, you can make additional tax-effective contributions into your superannuation in order to cover the cost of the premiums so that they do not erode your retirement savings.

SHOULD YOU CONTRIBUTE MORE?

Depending your life stage, it can be difficult to justify pouring large additional amounts of money into superannuation, as there may be many other things you want to do with your money between now and retirement. Nevertheless, the government is particularly keen for us to fund our own retirement and they have introduced some financial incentives to encourage us to do so. The main ones are:

- **Superannuation co-contribution**. By making a personal (after tax) contribution into your superannuation fund of up to $1000, the government may match this contribution by 150 per cent (up to $1500). The superannuation co-contribution applies if you are an employee, earning a wage and having superannuation paid by your employer, and are deemed to be a low-income earner. If this is you, the government will match by 150 per cent a personal superannuation contribution that you make into your superannuation fund, up to an amount of $1500.
- To be eligible for this maximum 150 per cent government contribution, you need to earn $28,000 or

less for the financial year (current in 2008). The percentage that the government contributes then shades out until your income reaches $58,000 per annum, when it stops. The ATO website has a great little co-contribution calculator at <www.ato.gov.au>. Getting a co-contribution can be a great way of paying for those insurance premiums—have the government do it for you!

An example

Assume that your income is $27,000 per annum. If you were to make a personal contribution of $500 into your superannuation fund, the government would contribute a further $750 on your behalf. If you were to contribute $1000 they would contribute $1500. If you contributed $2000 they would still only contribute $1500.

Assume your income is $40,000 per annum. Using the same figures as above, a personal contribution of $500 will still net you a co-contribution of $750. However, a $1000 contribution would only net you $900 as this is the maximum co-contribution the government is willing to pay you based on your income level.

Assume your income is $50,000 per annum. A personal contribution of $500 would net you a $400 co-contribution, as would any amount above this. Again, this is the maximum co-contribution the government will pay you based on your income level.

Please note that this is a very general overview of the co-contribution make sure you consult a professional before you undertake this strategy.

- **Spouse contribution into super**. Another way to boost your superannuation savings with the help of the government is to make an after-tax spouse contribution (a payment from your net income into the low income earner's superannuation fund). This can qualify your partner for an 18 per cent tax rebate.

If you will earn $10,800 assessable income or less for the financial year, and if you have a spouse, then your spouse can make a contribution into your superannuation fund and claim an 18 per cent tax rebate at the end of the financial year. The government will pay a rebate up to $540. The amount of rebate the government will pay fades out when you earn over $10,800, until it cuts out completely when your earnings hit $13,800.

An example
Assume that you earned $10,000 for the financial year and your spouse paid $2000 into your superannuation fund. The rebate would be 18 per cent of the $2000 ($360). If he paid $3000 the rebate would be $540. If he paid $4000 the rebate would still be $540 as this is the maximum. This rebate can be claimed at tax time.

Again, this is a very general overview and you should seek professional advice before doing this.

- **Salary sacrifice**. This is a way for higher income earners to effectively top up their superannuation tax. 'Salary sacrifice' is where you make a contribution to your superannuation fund from your gross salary—that is, your pre-tax salary. This enables you to potentially pay more into your superannuation than you are losing in your take home pay.

To elaborate, if you are a higher income earner then you will not be able to take advantage of the government co-contribution. And if you are both higher income earners you will not be able to take advantage of the spouse contribution either. But you can still make tax-effective superannuation contributions by using salary sacrifice. Keep in mind that pre-tax contributions made into your super fund (such as salary sacrifice and employer contributions) are charged a 'contributions tax' of 15 per cent by the fund. So a $1000 contribution will result in $850 being paid into your account. That is why salary sacrifice is most appropriate for higher income earners.

An example

Assume that you earn $50,000 and have a marginal tax rate of 30 per cent. A $1000 pre-tax contribution into your superannuation fund will only result in a $700 after-tax cost to you (because you would have paid $300 tax on the money before you received it otherwise). When the money goes into the fund it will be taxed at 15 per cent, your $1000 contribution will result in an $850 payment into your super. An overall saving of $150 in tax.

Same example but assume that you earn $100,000 and have a marginal tax rate of 40 per cent. A $1000 pre-tax contribution into your superannuation fund will only result in a $600 after-tax cost to you (because you would have paid $400 tax on the money before you received it otherwise). When the money goes into the fund it will be taxed at 15 per cent. So your $1000 contribution will result in an $850 payment into your super. An overall saving of $250 in tax.

Yet again, get professional advice before doing this.

These three strategies are great government incentives for putting money into superannuation. However, it's always important to weigh up the benefits with the fact that once money is in superannuation, it is generally locked in until you retire after the age of 60. This is a fairly big trade-off so don't leave yourself in financial hardship just to gain some government benefit.

CHAPTER SIXTEEN

VALUE YOURSELF

A good wife always knows her place.
The Good Wife's Guide

Actually I think that should read: 'A good wife always knows her worth.' A 2004 study by a couple of Swiss economists concluded that a happy marriage is worth US$100,000 a year. Apparently this is because getting married provides 'basic insurance against adverse life events and allows gains from economies of scale and specialisation within the family'. I'm not quite sure what those economies of scale and specialisations are, but it sounds impressive.

I can sort of understand how they could arrive at a figure like that. After all, without their wives, men would have to hire someone to cook, shop for food, clean the house, wash, iron the clothes, run errands and look after the kids. Possibly also someone to do the gardening and wash the cars. That may well cost more than $100,000 per year.

Without their husbands, women would have to hire someone to forget to put out the rubbish.

Of course, this $100,000 of value is in addition to the $50,000 of happiness that I mentioned in Chapter 2, that we create each year by having sex. We women are a very valuable bunch.

Financial Tip of the Week
Make the most of your greatest asset—you!

As I have very clearly demonstrated above, you are your greatest asset. I know that sounds obvious but it is easy to forget in the rush of day-to-day life. It's a fundamental truth—you are the greatest asset you have and you should take every opportunity to make the most of that asset.

I'm not just talking financially (even though financial management is the theme of *How to Afford a Husband*). I'm talking about in every way; physically, mentally and, yes, financially. It's all equally important and it's all interrelated. Just as a car needs its engine to be working as well as having good tyres and having fuel in the tank for it to run smoothly, you need all aspects of your life to be in order so that you can run smoothly too. It's a quality *and* quantity rationale.

Never stop learning. The discipline I imposed on myself was to work harder on myself than on my job … I drew from this the determination to educate myself, to discipline myself with my savings, to find mentors who could inspire me (including my boyfriends), to visit stimulating places, to read good books and listen to uplifting music and to go to as many motivational seminars as I could find about 'how to develop your self-esteem and self image', remembering I never knew the meaning of self-esteem and self image at school. Such a concept was beyond my comprehension.

Sarina Russo, founder and managing
director of the Sarina Russo Group.
Extract from her book, Meet Me at the Top

Let's look at it from a financial perspective. It is your combined incomes that pay for all the day-to-day expenses and it is your incomes that make your financial goals possible. Your incomes that build up your investments. And just as you want to get the optimal return on the investments that you have, you want to receive the optimal income as well. This might mean enhancing, or changing, your career.

Sometimes we may not be totally happy with our careers, but we lack the motivation to do anything about it. Get that motivation! You don't want to look back in 15 years and think 'if only'. Australia is a land of opportunity. There is no reason to be stuck in a dead-end job that you don't like because there has never been a better time to make the move to enhance your career, or take the plunge and change it altogether.

ENHANCING

Expanding your business or climbing the corporate ladder rarely happens by accident; it's generally by design. It is a matter of knowing what role you want and knowing what you need to do to get that role. It may be that you need to do some additional study or perhaps some additional work experience. There is no time like the present to find out more about these things.

First you need to decide what type of change you are looking for. Perhaps you love your chosen field of work but would like a more senior position? Perhaps you would prefer to move to a different department altogether? Perhaps you would like more supervisory responsibility or a more hands-on role? Whatever change it is, the chances are that you can put a plan in place to do it.

Once you have identified the role you want, write down the job description for that role and the qualifications and personal attributes you think would be needed for that role. Then write down what your current qualifications are and what you believe to be your personal strengths. From that you should be able to identify any gaps.

Then make a time to sit down with your employer and discuss with her how you can work together to make your desired career progression happen. Most employers will appreciate this sign of ambition and be more than happy to work with you to make it happen.

If it is a qualification that you need your employer may be able to let you know exactly what study is required. She may be able to provide the learning materials in-house or point you in the right direction. If you are lucky, she may even pay for it (otherwise it may be a tax deduction for you but check with the ATO).

If it is work experience you need, you may be able to come to some arrangement with your employer to get that experience, either through practical training or through hands-on work experience.

CHANGING

Perhaps you are not so much wishing to enhance your career as change it altogether—not so much a progression upwards but more a leap into uncharted waters. Many people have several career changes before they reach retirement. This can be for financial or lifestyle reasons. Either way, the days of working for one company from age 17 to 60 are, for most of us, long gone.

As I have said, there are jobs out there in many different fields. If you are a hairdresser who has always wanted to be a police officer, or a secretary who has always wanted to be an accountant, then it's a great time to put those wheels in motion.

Career changes don't happen overnight. They usually involve study and/or work experience and/or experience in a related field, so it's good to be fairly certain about the career change before you become immersed in study and work experience. Sometimes the grass may look greener in an alternative career, but looks can be deceiving.

Once you have identified the new career you want, write down the job description for that role and the qualifications and personal attributes you think would be needed for that role. If you are not sure about this, check some job advertisements or contact a recruitment company. Then write down what your current qualifications are and what you believe to be your personal strengths. From that you should be able to identify any gaps.

Once you know what the gaps are, work on closing them. As an example, you may have identified study that needs to be done. Start investigating where you can do that study and how much it will cost. Either work the cost into your goals or investigate whether you would qualify for Centrelink assistance. Centrelink has three main study-related payments available:

- Youth allowance
- Austudy A
- ABStudy

A detailed summary of each of these is payments beyond the scope of this book—you can look them up on the Centrelink website <www.centrelink.gov.au> or make an appointment to see a Centrelink information services officer.

Recruitment consultant Richard Dunks gives the following tips for people wanting to improve their marketability:

- Consider updating skills through volunteer work or doing some work with a not-for-profit organisation.
- Ensure your technical skills are kept up to date.

- Ensure that you are aware of any legislative changes or other industry changes in your field.
- Keep in touch with your employer and colleagues and keep updated with what is happening there. Richard calls this 'prevention, rather than starting from ground zero'.
- It's all about presentation: of your resumé, your phone manner and your physical appearance (remember to update that business wardrobe if it is out of date or non-existent).

Of course, enhancing or changing your career is not just about money. Lifestyle is even more important. You may want to downsize your role for a lower-paid one in the organisation that will give you greater job satisfaction or more flexible working hours. You may want to work part-time instead of full-time. Or you may want to change careers to something that has a lower salary.

A friend of mine threw in her job as an accountant to become a childcare worker—a role that doesn't pay anywhere near as well (although it should, as good childcarers play an extremely important role in shaping the future of our kids and they are worth their weight in gold). However, the point is that she loves going to work each day instead of waking up with that sinking 'damn, it's not the weekend' feeling.

By following the steps outlined so far—getting your goals written down, knowing what your financial situation is, having your budget and tracking system and savings in place—you will have the confidence to make this lifestyle change if you want to. You will not need to delay it for years, unsure about whether you can afford it or not (or convincing yourself that you can't). Instead, your finances will be under control and you will know exactly what is affordable and what isn't. Which is a very liberating thing.

CHAPTER SEVENTEEN

STARTING A BUSINESS

Don't complain if he's late home for dinner or
even if he stays out all night. Count this as
minor compared to what he might have gone
through that day.
The Good Wife's Guide

*I can't imagine that the reaction of most wives to their husband's
staying out all night would be 'minor compared to what he might
have gone through that day'. I'm trying to think of work-based
situations that could be worse for a man than having his crown jewels
kicked really hard by a stiletto-clad foot. I'm coming up blank.*

*And in any case, I'm not sure exactly what it is that the author
of* The Good Wife's Guide *assumed that husbands did at work
all day back then. Presumably, more than the average worker does
now.*

A British study recently found that the average employee has just four productive hours at work each day. The rest of the time is taken up with emails, phone calls and internet surfing. That's based on both men's and women's working habits.

I could do with far fewer work-based emails. While I appreciate an open flow of office-based communication, it is possible to have too much of a good thing. And text messages, quite frankly, are just puzzling. Perhaps it is because I'm a Gen X, but it takes me far longer to work out what 'Hi JD, jtlyk, imo 2moz we shd c a mve. Idk which 1 tho' means than it would for the texter to phone and say, 'Hey, want to catch a movie tomorrow? What should we see?'

And call me old fashioned, but when it comes to romance, an 'ilu' text isn't quite the same as telling someone you love them!

Financial Tip of the Week
Starting a business.

Sick of working for 'The Man/Woman'? Like the idea of striking out on your own—being answerable to no one but yourself? Or perhaps building up an empire of busy workers, all making a profit for you? If you take this tip, you will never have time for pointless emails again!

Running a business is an idea that appeals to a lot of people. According to the Australian Bureau of Statistics, of the approximately 13.4 million people in Australia who participate in the workforce, over 1.6 million are small business operators. That mean's around 12 per cent of the labour force participants are small business operators. In addition there are also a significant proportion of self-employed people not classed as small business owners; around 20 per cent of workers overall are not classed as employees.

> The nine to five 'man in the grey flannel suit', who stayed in one career in one company for a lifetime, has long been pronounced extinct. In this post-industrial era, we live in a fast-changing world with increasingly rich textured lifestyles, and in which work functions are continually altering. We combine roles and responsibilities as parents, executives, consultants, students, carers, volunteers, friends, personal and business partners. For most of us it's no longer possible to divide the world into three neat domains: work, home and play.
>
> —*Dr Jane Shelton, author of* No Workplace Like Home

Getting back to small businesses—72 per cent of small businesses are sole proprietors and around 67 per cent of small businesses are home based. There are a lot of advantages to having your own business, including the following:

- The most obvious, of course, is being your own boss.
- Being the decision maker.
- Being in charge of the day-to-day operations.
- No office politics.
- The flexibility of work hours.
- Having, to a certain extent, control over your income. (Hopefully, the harder you work the more you will earn.)

- Being able to achieve a work/life balance that may not be available in your place of employment (particularly useful if you have children).

There are numerous other advantages that may apply to your specific situation. Owning your own business can be an enjoyable and liberating experience.

It can also be time consuming, stressful and not at all financially rewarding, so you need to put some very serious thought into the nuts and bolts of the business before you take the plunge, to be quite certain that it really is the right decision for you.

What sorts of things do you need to think about? First and foremost, you need to decide what type of goods you are going to sell or what type of service you are going to provide. Depending on your current skills this may be a foregone conclusion—you may simply be branching out on your own via the field you already work in. Or you might want a complete sea change. Either way, you will need to be certain that there is a market for your product/service that you can tap into and that there are not too many players already in that market.

You also need to know what level of financial commitment the business will require from you. What are the set-up and ongoing costs of your business likely to be? The set-up costs can vary greatly, depending on whether you are setting up an actual shop or setting up a home-based service business. It is important not to underestimate the amount of financial commitment your business may require. Even a home-based business will need:

- A business bank account
- Advertising costs
- Stationery
- Phone/email/fax/photocopier and associated ongoing costs
- Business insurance
- Filing system
- Accounting software
- Trading stock.

Not to mention registering your business and paying your share of tax to the Tax Office along the way. These are just basic costs that all businesses would require. Additional costs will depend on the type of business you are setting up and the list could go on and on and on.

You also need to be aware of the amount of time commitment that your new business may require from you, particularly in the start-up phase. Building up and retaining a client base, promoting your business, keeping up to date with legislative changes and market trends, making sure you keep your own skill set up to date through training and research. Not to mention the actual running of the business to provide the goods or services in the first place (and attending to the associated administrative paperwork). You will discover that, from a business-owner point of view, there is no such thing as spare time.

I don't want to put a dampener on the idea of business ownership—I do half of my work from home and it's great—but it's important to be realistic about the cost and work that may be involved. According to Australian Bureau of Statistics figures, approximately 53 per cent of small businesses in Australia are less than five years old. Yet overall, the number of small businesses does not grow much from census to census. What that tells us is that a fair proportion of small businesses must stop trading each year, for whatever reason, in order to make way for more new start-ups. So go into your own business with your eyes open. Have a plan and a realistic idea of how much effort will be required to make your business successful.

Let's say you have decided to set up a business and work for yourself. You know what type of product/service you are going to offer and you are confident there is a market ready and waiting out there. Where to next? A basic step-by-step guide is as follows:

1. Decide what type of business structure you are going to set up. Are you going to be a sole trader or partnership, a company or a trust? The different business structures have varying registration and taxation implications. Your relevant state government will have a website to guide you through this decision. For example, check <www.smallbiz.nsw.gov.au>. The Tax Office also puts out a booklet, *Tax Basics for Small Business,* which can be downloaded from their website <www.ato.gov.au>.

2. Find out what is legally required to register your business. You may need to register a business name with the Office of Fair Trading or, if you are setting up a company, you may need to register the company with the Australian Securities and Investment Commission

(ASIC). You may also need a separate tax file number, depending on the business structure you decide on.

3. What business-related insurance do you need? For example, you may require professional indemnity insurance and public liability insurance.

4. Do you require any particular licences to run your business?

5. Register for an Australian Business Number (ABN) and familiarise yourself with the types of taxes you may be required to pay. You may also need to register for GST. Again, refer to the ATO's booklet, *Tax Basics for Small Business*.

6. Are there any council restrictions on you running your business of choice from your premises of choice?

These are just the really basic before-you-even-start-getting-serious things you need to investigate. Once you have crossed those molehills you can start looking at the figurative mountain of setting up a business plan and making sure that it all (financially and from a lifestyle point of view) stacks up.

The Australian government has set up a great website <www.business.gov.au> which is an invaluable source of information for anyone considering business ownership. As part of this website they take you through setting up a business plan and even provide business plan templates. In the same way as setting up a written budget will help you control your expenditure, setting up a written business plan will help you control your business. The website also contains an excellent checklist for starting a business, called, strangely enough, *Checklist for Starting a Business*. This website also contains links to many other state-based websites that might be relevant to you and your ideas of starting up a business.

Even if you are buying an existing business or a franchise you still need to put the same amount of care into having a written business plan. In addition, you need to carefully investigate whether the business is worth buying in the first place. That is, if the business is so good then why is it for sale? Or if the franchise is such a great idea then why hasn't it already been snapped up in your area? You want to make sure you are getting value for money.

Part of your plan will include financial projections for your business. So once you have your business plan and have mapped out what you conservatively expect your ongoing cash flow to look like, you need to compare your before- and after-tax cash flow with your current employee cash flow (your salary) to make sure that you will definitely be better off by running your own business. Do this as follows:

Business $	Employee $	Difference $
Estimated cash flow	Estimated salary	
Less costs	Plus fringe benefits	
	Plus bonuses	
Less tax	Less tax	
Net cash flow	Net cash flow	
	Plus superannuation	
	Plus other benefits	
	(e.g. employee shares,	
	discounts)	
Total cash in hand		

Hopefully, your business column will earn as much, if not more money than your employee column. If not it doesn't necessarily mean that the business is a bad idea—there may be other trade-offs that make it worthwhile—but knowing the financial wash-up is very important.

The next thing to do is look at the lifestyle comparison. Again, put it into a table:

Advantages of business	Advantages of being employed
Being your own boss	Having a guaranteed income
Flexibility of work hours	Having paid sick leave
Being able to combine work with parenting	Having paid holiday leave
Building a brand that will be valuable in the future	
	Training and career development provided in-house
Monetary reward for hard work	Having superannuation and other financial employee benefits
No office politics	Companionship of colleagues

I am sure that you can think of many more advantages of each structure—you will know what is important to you. Don't forget to include your partner in this as your decision will impact on their financial and lifestyle future as well. They can probably add their own set of advantages to the above list.

I am also a big supporter of getting professional advice on just about any aspect of your life, and setting up a business is no exception. Once you have done your research, consider making an appointment with a business adviser as well as with your accountant (again, check your state government website for referrals to business advisory services). Go through your plans with them and get the full benefit from their professional expertise. Then make it happen.

CHAPTER EIGHTEEN

DONATE

Make him comfortable. Have him lean back
in a comfortable chair or have him lie down in
the bedroom. Have a cool or warm drink
ready for him.
The Good Wife's Guide

The more of these 'Good Wife' quotes I read, the more I am coming to the conclusion that what I would really like is a wife of my own. Either that or a personal concierge. Come to think of it, a concierge might be less hassle.

If I ever won Lotto, the very first thing I would do is hire a personal concierge. Forget about flashy cars and big houses—at the end of the day they're just extra things to maintain. What I really want is someone always on hand to maintain the stuff that we already have. How incredibly good would that be?

Someone who could cook, who could whip up a light and tasty something on a whim. Someone who maintained my wardrobe so that whatever I wanted to wear that day would always be clean and pressed. If they could also double as a personal stylist that would be even better. They could flick through the fashion magazines, give me a written summary of the season's trends, then go and buy them for me.

They could make my dinner reservations, answer my correspondence and maintain my diary. They could free up my time to go to the gym, read the books I want to read and do the 'fun stuff' that I currently just don't have the time for. Bliss!

Financial Tip of the Week
Donate regularly—it helps to keep things in perspective.

Ah well, back to the real world. And when I compare my situation to that of many other people in that real world, what the heck would I need a concierge for? I live in Australia in security and comfort. I have a nice roof over my head, a healthy family, the ability to earn an income and the prospect of a happy future. In the eyes of a huge proportion of the world's population, I've already hit the jackpot.

As we all have. Donating regularly is probably a strange tip for a money management book, but making regular donations from your hard-earned cash is a great way to keep your lifestyle, your priorities and your spending in perspective.

As I have mentioned, we are constantly bombarded with

advertisements for wonderful things to buy. This constant bombardment can make it very easy to lose your perspective on what really are the important things in life.

Australia is a fairly materialistic society (though not as bad as some) and being constantly told about all the material things that we 'really must have' can be incredibly stressful. It's a never-ending treadmill. We're constantly working harder and harder to earn more and more, just to buy stuff that we don't really need, until we realise we are losing the genuinely valuable things in our life—our relationships, our health and our youth. Sometimes we need to step off the treadmill and take a look at the big wide world to get a dose of needed reality. Donating to a charity is a great way to do this.

Ongoing world problems don't often make the news. Sure, a bomb explosion or plane crash will score a headline but the daily pain, such as the estimated 30,000 children who die every day as a result of poverty and preventable disease, doesn't.

Think about setting yourself a goal to cut $10 per week from your grocery bill and use this money as a regular monthly donation to a charity of your choice. That's about $43 per month: you could sponsor a child through World Vision for that, or provide 278 tourniquets or 80 sterile burns dressings through Medecins Sans Frontiers. There are plenty of other opportunities to make a difference out there and it's not too hard to find them. Becoming involved with a charity, receiving their newsletters and articles will help keep your perspective after a hard day on the consumer treadmill.

From a financial point of view, monetary donations are also a tax deduction. You can maximise the amount of refund the Tax Office provides by making the donation in the name of the highest income earner in your family.

CHAPTER NINETEEN

HOUSE HUNTING

Remember, he is the master of the house and,
as such, will always exercise his will
with fairness and truthfulness.
The Good Wife's Guide

Amazing, with all that exercising of will that the 'master of the house' so often ends up with a floral bedspread.

If there is one thing that proves beyond a doubt that men are not masters of their domain, it's the way that their home is usually decorated; generally it's feminised. Artfully arranged fake flowers, designer cushions scattered in precise random locations and curtains that match the feature wall perfectly. Most men couldn't give a toss what colour the curtains are, so long as they don't have to tramp around the shops finding them.

There are exceptions to this rule (and my own home is a case in point), but by and large it seems to be the female who decides how the interior of a house should look. Not that males are excluded entirely from the decision-making process. Quite often they get to organise the shed. And sometimes even the toilet (the one that the guests won't see).

Financial Tip of the Week
Buying a house.

The Real Estate Institute of Queensland (REIQ) encourages anyone who can afford it to buy property to secure their long-term future. However, they must be able to afford the property and the ongoing costs.

One of the characteristics of Australians is that we prefer to own rather than rent. We have one of the highest rates of home ownership in the world and that's part of our unique character as Australians.

—*Dan Molloy, managing director, REIQ*

Note that I have put 'buying', not 'buy'. The object here is to weigh up the pros and cons of buying a house, as opposed to renting and investing the remainder of your money elsewhere.

I should say from the outset that I am strongly in favour of people buying their own home to live in. Cameron and I have our own house (to be perfectly frank the bank owns our house; we just live in it and hand over an obscene amount of mortgage repayment each month) and we have enjoyed not only the rise in property values over the last few years but also the psychological value that comes from owning our own place and being a permanent part of the local community.

Nevertheless, home ownership is not for everyone and you are not necessarily financially disadvantaged by renting—provided that you invest the money that would otherwise be going towards the mortgage and other house-related costs.

It is a financial question that various newspapers and magazines like to pose from time to time: are you financially better off renting and investing elsewhere, or buying? Generally, by the time all the costs of each option are taken into account, and depending on what growth figures are used, the papers will conclude either that you are marginally better off renting or marginally better off buying. The word to note is 'marginally'—in other words, it usually works out roughly about the same.

So what are the main pros and cons—or advantages and disadvantages—of owning your own home? Let's look at the advantages first:

ADVANTAGES OF OWNING YOUR OWN HOME

- Paying a mortgage is a form of enforced saving because it is compulsory; this mortgage repayment is money that you can't spend on something else.
- With each mortgage repayment you make you own a little bit more of your property outright. As time goes on you can potentially borrow against this ownership for other investments (refer back to gearing in Chapter 14).

- Unlike other investments, your home is exempt from capital gains tax.
- Apart from financial benefits, there are personal benefits in owning your own home, including the freedom to renovate and redecorate.
- You are more likely to feel part of a neighbourhood community by owning the house you live in.
- There is a greater sense of permanency about your living arrangements; your tenancy is not at the whim of a landlord.

All great stuff but there are also some disadvantages to owning your own home. Some of the more common ones are:

DISADVANTAGES OF OWNING YOUR OWN HOME

- It costs a lot! Not just the mortgage repayments, which in themselves could be up to 30 per cent of your income, but all the other initial costs such as legals and stamp duty, mortgage application fees and so on.
- As well as all the initial fees there are plenty of regular ongoing fees, including rates, maintenance and repairs.
- Having a house can geographically tie you down. It's more difficult to move interstate or overseas if you have a house and mortgage repayments to consider.
- Having to make large mortgage repayments at this time of your life can also limit other study and career opportunities that you may have.

- You might not be able to afford to buy in the area where you want to live (whereas you may be able to afford to rent in that area).
- It's harder to move if you decide that you really don't like the area (or the neighbours).

So there are some pros and cons to owning your own place. How about renting and investing the financial difference?

ADVANTAGES OF RENTING AND INVESTING

- There is less compulsory financial outlay upfront. This means that potentially there are funds left over to help you achieve other personal and career goals.
- You can have a more diversified spread of investments. Rather than all your savings being tied up in one house, you can spread your money across a range of different investments such as shares, property and cash (refer back to Chapter 12 for a summary of these different investments).
- If you don't like the neighbourhood or neighbours, it's quite easy to simply pack up and move.
- Many of the ongoing expenses and maintenance associated with the property are your landlord's responsibility, not yours. This makes it easier to budget for exactly how much your accommodation is going to cost you.
- Borrowings may be tax deductible. Any money that you borrow to invest, as opposed to borrowing for a mortgage, are generally tax deductible. For example, if

you took out a margin loan to buy some shares, the interest charged on that margin loan would be a tax deduction.

- You may be able to afford to rent in an area that really appeals to you whereas a mortgage in that same area might be unaffordable.

DISADVANTAGES OF RENTING AND INVESTING

- Not investing the excess funds. While your intentions may be pure, it is very easy to simply spend the difference between mortgage repayments and rent. Unless you are investing the difference you will be going backwards financially.
- Whereas the real cost of a mortgage will decrease over time (that is, the mortgage repayments may start out being 30 per cent of your income, after a few years as your income rises the same dollar amount of repayments will be a lesser percentage of your income), rental payments will keep increasing.
- Your life may be disrupted as you will probably move house more often. This can be fun when you are young and childless, but it is a nuisance once you have a family.

There are lots of other little advantages and disadvantages that will depend upon you and your personality and your preference.

Let's assume that you have decided to buy a house. What do you need to do to prepare yourself for this big step?

1. Know how much you can spend. First and foremost, you need to find out approximately how much you can borrow. Most financial institutions will have an online borrowings calculator to help you work this out. As a general rule of thumb, they generally like to keep repayments to less than 30 per cent of your gross income (anything above that is considered mortgage stress).

2. Once you know how much you will likely borrow and what your monthly repayments will be, get out your budget (the one we did in Chapter 4) and rework it (add in the mortgage repayments, add in annual property expenses such as rates and maintenance, take out your rental costs) to make sure that your proposed spending amount is going to be affordable.

3. When you know roughly how much you can spend on a property you can work out what geographical areas you should be targeting. Position, as always, is the most important thing to consider. It's much better from a financial point of view to have the worst-looking house in the best street as opposed to the best-looking house in the worst street. Do your homework in the areas that you are considering—and find out what comparative properties have sold for in the recent months.

4. Check your credit rating. Do this before you approach the financial institution, as you don't want any nasty surprises when you apply for your loan. ASIC's consumer website has some useful information on what credit ratings are and how to find yours. Check their website <www.fido.asic.gov.au>.

5. If you are a first home buyer you may be eligible for some government benefit, such as the first home buyers grant. Check out your entitlements on <www.firsthome.gov.au>. Additionally, you may receive other state-based first home buyer benefits— you will need to check these on your relevant state's website (the <www.firsthome.gov.au> website contains links to the various state government websites).

6. Know what other costs you may be up for when buying a house. These costs will also need to be worked into your budget (or taken out of your savings) and could include:
   • Stamp duty
   • Mortgage insurance
   • Loan application fees
   • Valuation fees
   • Solicitor's fees
   • Search fees
   • Building and pest reports
   • Insurance of home and contents.

7. Make an appointment to sit down with your banking specialist. Not only should they be able to advise you about the costs listed above, they will be able to advise you on the types of home loans available to you and the interest rates payable.

8. If you are thinking of buying a property at auction then discuss this with your banker beforehand. Properties sold at auction are sold 'unconditional', which means you will need to have your finance approved before you bid. You will also need to have a

deposit of 5 to 10 per cent ready to hand over on the day of the auction.

If you decide not to buy a house but want to set up an equivalent investment portfolio instead, then follow these guidelines:

1. Go through steps 1 and 2 on page 185 and work out how much you would likely borrow for a mortgage and what the associated costs of borrowing would be. Add to this the estimated annual maintenance and other costs of holding the property (for example, rates, capital expenditure). Work this out to a monthly amount.

2. Subtract the cost of your rent from the amount you have tallied above. This will give you the monthly amount that you should be investing in order to be keeping pace. So, for example, if your mortgage repayments and other monthly home-ownership costs would be $3000, and your monthly rent is $1200, then the amount that you should be investing each month is $1800. This amount should encompass whatever you invest, the ongoing costs of the investment plus the after-tax cost of any investment borrowings that you make.

3. Re-read Chapter 12 to refresh your memory on the types of assets and investments that are available.

4. Make an appointment to see a financial planner. A financial planner will provide you with advice on what types of investments may be suitable for you, given

your individual situation, and can assist you in setting up an investment portfolio. They can also manage this for you on an ongoing basis. Friends or colleagues may be able to refer you to a financial planner, or alternatively the Financial Planning Association's website <www.fpa.asn.au> contains a 'find a planner' tool for all suburbs. This will list planners who are members of the association.

Whichever way you decide to go, ideally it should be for the long term. Having said that, nothing is ever set in concrete. If you do take the plunge one way or the other and find in a few years that you want to do something different—fine. As the Nike ad says: 'Just do it'.

CHAPTER TWENTY

SPLITTING UP

If the socially unthinkable should happen and
your husband requests a divorce, accede his
request with good grace and apologise for the
inconvenience caused to him. Accept full
responsibility for driving him away.
The Good Wife's Guide

*Just kidding—I made that one up. But I'm sure the original author
would have included it if they had thought of it.*

*And it can be so difficult when friends break up. How do you
handle it? What do you say? And how do you offer sympathetic
support without taking sides?*

*In some ways it's far easier if only one member of the couple
is your friend. That way it's easy to be fully supportive,
encouraging and sympathetic to your friend's angst-ridden*

analysis of the (former) relationship. While offering support to your friend it's wise to avoid comments like 'we could all see it coming' or 'there's much better options out there' or even 'what the hell were you doing going out with that loser for so long anyway?' Even if it is meant in a positive way, comments like these merely make the point to your friend that she has hopeless taste in men, wastes herself on losers and is completely blind to the fact that you all feel sorry for her. And if they do get back together your comments could bite you on the proverbial. Not only will your friend know exactly how low your opinion of her partner is, she will probably tell him as well.

These minor issues of tact pale into insignificance when compared to the scenario of where a couple, both of whom are your friends, break up. What are you supposed to do? How do you offer support equally to both? Or do you regulate your amount of support based on who was at fault?

Furthermore, how do you handle future social situations? Do you invite them both to every party, or take it in turns to invite one? And what about their new boyfriends/girlfriends—are you open about your friendship with the 'ex', or do you never mention it? It can be very tricky.

Financial Tip of the Week
Handling separation.

Not a nice topic to cover but unfortunately it's something that does happen a fair bit. Almost one in two marriages in Australia end in divorce and a lot of relationships don't even make it that far.

This chapter doesn't deal with all the legal or emotional issues surrounding divorce (those two things would each take another book). This chapter is simply a basic overview of the main financial issues that you will need to think about, both together and separately. It is also not meant to replace getting professional advice, which you should do as a matter of priority. Hopefully, the information here will point you in the right direction to seek that advice.

It doesn't matter whether you have been married for 10 years or living together unmarried for two. If you are sharing finances and have joint financial commitments, then there is a level of financial settlement that you need to attend to. Obviously the more straightforward your situation—both personally and financially—the simpler it will be to finalise your financial settlement. If you have been married for a number of years, have children or a business together or substantial assets and debts, the situation can get more complicated.

When it comes to considering the cost of separation, the sky's the limit—well almost. If you opt for a do-it-yourself separation you could get out of it for under $1000. On the other hand if you need the courts to assess your situation and make the decision for you, your legal costs could be $10,000 upwards (and sometimes *much* higher). I am not saying that you must seek legal and accounting advice but depending on your situation you could end up financially much worse off by not seeking professional advice.

Optimistically any separation would be amicable and you would both have enough respect for and trust of each other not to try taking advantage of or revenge against your partner. However, it's easy when you are happily together with no thought of separation to nod and agree that, yes, in the event of a break-up everything would be very civil. This could change, depending upon the reason for the break-up.

> One day you are part of a couple. Sure you argue a bit, who doesn't, but you are sharing responsibilities like kids or mortgage and you come home to each other at night. You have always managed to sort through your problems before and you have no reason to think this time was any different. Then BAM: someone said those fateful words that ended it.
>
> Your marriage may have ended through indifference or through an affair or maybe just because it got too hard for one of you. Whatever the reason, it is over and you are stunned. Your marriage is finished. The big question is: what do you do about it?
>
> —*Lynette Galvin, accredited family law specialist*

It's important to always be aware of what your financial situation is so that in the event of splitsville you will not be in for any nasty surprises. In government-terrorism-awareness-type talk, you should always be alert but not alarmed.

What do I mean by this? Remember all the way back in Chapter 2 we went through and mapped out your current financial situation? It's something that you should do periodically and it's something that you should refer to fairly promptly in the event of separation. In fact, not to sound too callous, you should refer to it immediately the door closes behind him forever. Pay special attention to the 'OWNER' column on the spreadsheet. How many of your financial assets are held in joint names? I'm talking about things like bank accounts, savings account, credit cards and so on. Be aware (but not alarmed) that if something is owned or owed jointly, it does not mean that you own/owe half of that item each. What it means is that you are both considered to own/owe all of that item together.

In other words, if you have a $5000 bank account held jointly, this does not mean you each own $2500. It means that you each have access to $5000 of cash. Unless you have a two-signatory requirement on withdrawals, the bank will be happy to let you withdraw $5000 and will be equally happy to allow your partner to withdraw $5000. Likewise with a joint credit card, the credit card company will be happy for either of you to run up debt to the limit of the card and will not distinguish between you when demanding repayment.

It's wise to take steps to secure the assets that you have at the time of the separation. I know it may be the last thing in the world that you feel like doing in the first 24 hours after your partner leaves, but it's better to delay the day sobbing under the doona or the 24-hour drinking marathon with friends until tomorrow. Otherwise you may be sobbing or drinking away your sorrows for more than one reason. Grab a manila folder and take a snapshot of what exists at the time of separation. For example, print out a statement of account balances (including credit cards) from your internet banking and get current balances for any other investments faxed or emailed to you.

If you have a joint bank account, perhaps withdraw half the balance and place the funds into an account solely in your name. If you have a joint credit card, put a stop on the card for the time being (make sure you tell your partner in advance that you are going to do this). Change your internet banking password. Photocopy any relevant financial paperwork belonging to either of you. Try not to overlook anything. Assets/liabilities that you may have and want copies of include:

Assets
- Bank accounts
- Savings accounts
- Managed funds
- Shares
- House title
- Investment property titles
- Superannuation (yours and his)
- Family trusts
- Business assets
- Car registration
- Insurance policies
- Take a copy of the previous year's tax returns for each of you.

Liabilities
- Mortgage agreements
- Credit cards
- Car loans
- Any other personal loans
- Investment loans (for property, shares or managed funds)

- Estimates of any other outstanding liabilities (for example, a tax bill)
- Don't forget any debts that may be in your partner's name but on which you have gone guarantor—you are just as liable as he is for these debts.

As I said, it sounds callous but it can help to reduce any conflict or misunderstanding between you and your ex-partner down the track when who owned what at the time of separation might be hotly debated.

Once you have taken care of the above, *then* go out and celebrate/commiserate with your friends. After you have recovered from your hangover you can investigate in more detail the process of separation, divorce and property settlement.

Depending on the complexity of your situation you may need a lawyer and an accountant to help you work through the financial implications of your separation. And don't leave your financial planner out of the loop. If you and your partner both use the same accountant and financial planner it's probably best to ask for a referral to another professional as you don't want any conflict of interest. Your financial planner can go through the investments that you currently have. Your accountant can go through the cash flow and taxation statements for your personal and business situations and your lawyer can analyse the information to determine how your property settlement should be structured. All three professionals will probably want copies of the documents relating to your current financial situation.

In order to apply for divorce a couple must have been

separated for 12 months. After the 12 months has expired either party can file an application for divorce with the Federal Magistrates Court and usually about one month later a divorce order will take effect. Divorce in Australia is considered to be 'no-fault' and the only grounds for divorce is irretrievable breakdown of marriage.

Divorce is simply the legal process of dissolving a marriage and is quite separate to the issue of property settlement. Property settlement is the division of property. Assuming that you are married, the process is done through *The Family Law Act*. You and your partner can either both reach agreement yourselves about the division of your property (hopefully with the assistance of your accountant and lawyer) and request the court to make a consent order formalising this agreement. If you are unable to reach an agreement you can request the court to make a property settlement on your behalf.

Factors that will be considered by your lawyer (or the court if you have requested a court settlement) include:

- The financial and non-financial (such as housework, caring for children, etc.) contributions you have each made to the partnership.
- The potential earning power of each of you, in addition to the effect that the marriage has had on your earning power.
- Your health.
- Any other available financial resources (such as superannuation).
- The length of the marriage.

If you have children, the process will also involve some other steps. It's outside the scope of this chapter to deal with the legal and financial issues relating to children and separation, however, your lawyer will be able to advise you on these. Your first port of call should be the Family Assistance Office <www.familyassist.gov.au> as they can guide you through the payments available for sole parents and advise you on child support procedures.

Instead of the court process, you and your partner can choose to make a financial agreement relating to the division of your property and any ongoing maintenance. This type of agreement bypasses the court system. It must be drawn up with the help of your lawyers and must be signed by both parties to acknowledge that independent legal advice has been received. It is a binding agreement although it can be set aside by the court.

If you are de facto but not married, then the above information does not apply to you. A de facto situation is more complex as the property settlements are dealt with in the state courts and the law in each state differs. Having said that, it is a broadly similar approach to the division of property. Obtaining legal advice is the best option as your lawyer can take you through the property settlement process in your state.

Irrespective of whether you are married or de facto, please note that all this information is only a very general overview of how the process of separation works for couples. It certainly doesn't replace getting advice, although it should point you in the right direction for getting together all the information that your advisers may need.

Separation can be an extremely emotional and distressing time for you. Not only are you trying to deal with the loss of a relationship, you are being pressured into making all sorts of potentially large financial decisions. You may also be in the middle of having to move house, find furniture, even buy a new car. Not to mention the (sometimes unwelcome) sympathy and opinion of family and friends with regards to your break-up. It can be like living in the eye of a storm.

Never hesitate to seek counselling. Professional counselling can help you through the separation and settlement period, and help clear your head in order to make some of those large decisions. There are a number of counselling services available and you will need to search to find one that suits you and your situation. It is even better if you can source someone by a referral. A great government website to browse is <www.familyrelationships.gov.au>.

Receiving counselling can help you stay calm and rational throughout the process of separation. The more calm and rational you are, the less likely you will be to waste your hard-earned savings unnecessarily (easier said than done).

Once you have managed to get your head around all of the things that you have to do, you will need to revisit Chapters 4 and 5 (doing a budget and tracking system) as a matter of urgency as you will need a new budget to cater for your new (probably reduced) household income. You have probably just dropped from two incomes to one with maybe two-thirds of your previous expenses. You have taken steps to protect your savings from your partner and now you need to protect those hard-earned savings from yourself.

Once the legal and financial dust has settled you will need to revisit Chapters 2 through to 10, to get yourself set up as a single person. Part of that will involve reviewing the beneficiaries on your superannuation and insurance policies and redoing your will. Don't hesitate to get some financial counselling if the task seems too overwhelming to tackle alone—it is never an admission of failure to seek help. As the old clichéd saying goes, 'Failure is not falling down, it's staying down instead of getting up again'.

CHAPTER TWENTY-ONE

HAVING KIDS

> Prepare the children. Take a few minutes
> to wash the children's hands and faces
> (if they are small), comb their hair and, if
> necessary, change their clothes. They are little
> treasures and he would like to see them
> playing the part.
> *The Good Wife's Guide*

As a parent of three children under five, I will readily admit that I just can't believe how much I love my kids. They definitely are little treasures, however, they are also occasionally other descriptive things beginning with 'little'.

The children of complete strangers can sometimes also be other descriptive things beginning with 'little'. Particularly if they are kicking the back of my seat on a train/bus/plane or in a movie theatre. Or throwing a massive tantrum at the table next to me in a restaurant. Even more so if they have soiled their nappy and are sitting within smelling distance of me.

If I have managed to escape the clutches of my own brood for a day or an evening (it doesn't happen often), I would be prepared to pay a significant premium for the pleasure of not being seated somewhere close to anyone else's treasures. What price for a peaceful evening? I'm not sure, but around 20 per cent extra would be my guess.

Financial Tip of the Week
Starting a family.

Don't take my comments above the wrong way—kids are great. Starting a family is a hugely exciting time of life. It's important to realise that there is no 'best time' to have kids. You just do it when it feels right. I have written in my previous book, *How to Afford a Baby*, that I have seen clients delay having children in order to wait until they were more financially secure only to have to go through (expensive and traumatic) IVF later on. I have also seen clients struggle financially because they haven't put enough thought into the 'affording a baby' process. The trick is to strike a happy balance between the two extremes.

Whatever your career or material status, the thing that is going to create a happy household for you and your kids is not having vast amounts of money, but rather, managing the money that you do have, well.

Starting a family is undoubtedly the biggest decision you will ever make, it is the catalyst for so many other and sometimes difficult financial decisions you will need to consider over the course of raising your family. Besides the physical changes, whether it be the shape of your body to the scattered sleeping patterns you will soon enjoy, there are other changes far more difficult to come to terms with, such as going from two incomes down to one. If you decide to return to work there are still financial issues to consider such as the cost of childcare and the cost of going back to work, running a second car, work clothing and so on. For many of us, starting a family starts the ball rolling on a number of new financial challenges and pressures. It is financial concerns rather than the sounds of an unsettled baby that can keep you up at night. To lessen the financial burden, it is a good idea to seek advice, visit your financial planner, identify the more important financial considerations you will need to make. Do you have income protection? Who will the kids go to in an undue event, how will you cope on one wage? What school do you plan to send your child too, and more importantly, will you be able to afford it?

—*Sonia Williams, editor of* Show Mummy the Money
magazine

Babies can cost a lot of money. Even if you are lucky enough to have a whole lot of pre-loved family equipment available to you and would not, in a million years, dream of forking out for designer cots, prams and other paraphernalia, babies can still be expensive little bundles, out of all proportion to their size. If you are thinking of starting a family, there are some sensible financial strategies that you should put in place to ensure that you can easily afford to start a family and that you won't need to be financially stressed once you have.

1. Review the goals that we set up in Chapter 3—do they need to be altered?
2. Make a list of pregnancy-related costs you will have. Things such as medical expenses and scans, maternity clothes, antenatal courses and exercise classes. Don't forget any hospital excess you may have to pay, and allow money for things like extra physio and doctor visits (you just never know what sort of pregnancy you will have).
3. Make a list of baby-related costs. There is so much baby stuff out there to buy—some of it necessary, some of it completely unnecessary but subject to slick marketing campaigns. You will need a bare minimum, including cot, maybe a portable cot, bedding, baby capsule/car seat, pram, change mat or table, toy box, shelving, nappy bag, bottles, an initial supply of nappies and toiletries, some clothes (although not too many as you will probably be given lots of clothes). These are just the essentials and there is an entire *world* of baby-related equipment and accessories out there just waiting for you to discover it.
4. Allocate some of your savings to paying for all of the above.

5. Investigate your employee benefits well in advance. In addition to basic unpaid maternity leave, does your employer offer any paid maternity leave? Do you have any accrued holiday leave or long service leave that you could put into your melting pot of money? Is your partner entitled to any paternity leave, paid or unpaid?

6. Investigate the available government benefits. At the time of writing the main benefits that are available to most people are the lump sum maternity payment and the Family Tax Benefits (FTB) parts A and B. You can check out the details of these on the Family Assistance Office website <www.familyassist.gov.au>.

7. Do a budget, similar to the one set up in Chapter 4, based on what you estimate your monthly living expenses to be during the time that you will be on maternity leave. Some work-related expenses may reduce but other baby and lifestyle-related expenses will increase.

8. Determine how long you wish to take off work as maternity leave or if you want to go back at all. Be generous with the amount of maternity leave you allocate, as having a new baby is an incredibly special time of life that you won't want to miss.

9. Add up your partner's income (assuming that he is not stopping work), the employer and government benefits you will be eligible for plus any other income you will receive while on maternity leave. Divide this by the number of months you want to take off work. This will tell you what your monthly income shortfall will be between the amount of money coming in and the

amount of money going out each month. This total shortfall is the amount that you need to save between the time you become pregnant and the time you finish work. Let's look at an example so all of this makes sense.

The goal is to take 12 months' maternity leave.

Source	Amount $	Multiplied by	Total
Partner's monthly income	$5,000	12	$60,000
Holiday leave	$3,000		$3,000
Govt maternity payment	$5,000		$5,000
FTB part A	$80 p/f	26	$2,080
FTB part B	$45 p/f	26	$1,170
Total income			$71,250
Less monthly expenses	$6,800 p/m	12	$81,600
Shortfall			$10,350

According to the above example, your aim will be to save approximately $10,000 by the time you stop work in order to afford taking 12 months off. If you both applied the savings plan tips in Chapter 7 you will both be savings gurus by now and this won't be a problem for you. If the amount does seem unattainable, you may need to redirect some of your savings for other goals into this one.

Okay, we haven't finished yet.

Review your insurances (such as life, TPD, income protection and trauma cover), taking into consideration that your family is about to expand.

Review your estate planning in the same way.

Holy heck, what a lot to do! Of course, my most important tip if you are entering this stage of life is to buy a copy of *How to Afford a Baby*!

It all sounds very onerous, I know, but having a baby and enjoying their first months of development is one of the most wonderful experiences you will ever have. Of course there are the sleepless nights, the endless feeds and the unexplained crying to deal with, but overall, it's a great experience. You don't want it to be spoiled by niggling stress over finances.

CONCLUSION

There's a fine line between fishing and just
standing on the shore like an idiot.
Steven Wright, comedian

What an absolute bucketload of information we have
gone through! If you have both worked towards
implementing the financial tips in each chapter together,
you have set yourself up with some excellent financial
habits that will hold you in good stead and enhance the
quality of your life, both personally and together, for years
to come.

You have learned to recognise and respect each other's
financial motivations and viewpoint and have learned to
compromise or live with the differences. Differences are not
necessarily a bad thing—they keep you both on your toes—
as long as you know how to agree to disagree when
required.

You have set up some goals together and, more importantly, have set up a strategy for achieving them so that they are not just pie in the sky dreams. You have learned how to control your finances through budgeting and tracking your expenses, not to mention keeping your credit cards under control.

Once you know how much you spend, you can work out where to save money and we have looked at some of the more common budgeting strategies—areas where you can cut back your expenses without cutting back your quality of life. Once you know how much you spend you are also able to start saving with a clear conscience, to help you achieve those goals you have listed.

When you have your day-to-day finances under control, you can look at ensuring your future quality of life through insurance and estate planning. Once you are able to manage your day-to-day money you will have the solid foundations to be able to build future wealth through investment, either with your own money or via borrowing. You will also be able to take advantage of government superannuation incentives because you will have the available cash to do so.

All of these disciplines will enable you to weather any of life's unexpected storms, such as pregnancy or separation. It will also give you far greater self-confidence to branch out into a new career or enhance an existing one.

Most importantly, it will help to remove day-to-day financial stress from your life; a major source of conflict between couples. Yes, there will be bills to pay and deadlines to meet and an occasional overdrawn account when communication breaks down or something unexpected happens. With your big picture view that will be minor stuff, easy to work around, rather than it being an ignition point for a full-blown argument. You still will be on that riverbank of life, but you really will be fishing rather than standing there like an idiot.

APPENDIX I

In 2005, the federal government established the Financial Literacy Foundation. They commissioned a research report to gain an understanding of the financial attitudes, beliefs and practices of Australians. The questions below are some of those that they asked survey responders to gauge their attitudes, beliefs and behaviours about money. Try this questionnaire to put down on paper what you and your partner's attitude to money is. There are no right or wrong answers but this is a handy tool to help identify areas where you and your partner might clash.

QUESTIONS	Yes	Maybe	No
Dealing with money is stressful and overwhelming.	☐	☐	☐
Thinking too much about my long-term financial future makes me uncomfortable.	☐	☐	☐
Dealing with money is boring.	☐	☐	☐
I have the ability to understand financial language.	☐	☐	☐
At this point in my life it's important to learn more about how to understand financial language.	☐	☐	☐
Money is juts a means to buy things.	☐	☐	☐
Money is important to be happy in life.	☐	☐	☐
Financially, I like to live for today.	☐	☐	☐
I spend a lot of time thinking about financial information before I make a financial decision.	☐	☐	☐
I try to stay informed about money matters and finances.	☐	☐	☐
Nothing I do will make a big difference to my financial situation.	☐	☐	☐

APPENDIX 2

BALANCE SHEET

ASSETS	$ VALUE	LIABILITIES	$ VALUE
House		Mortgage 1	
Collectables/art		Mortgage 2	
Bank account 1		Overdraft	
Bank account 2		Credit cards	
Term deposits		Store cards	
Managed funds*		Car loan	
Shares		Other personal loans	
Investment property		Investment loan 1	
Other investments		Investment loan 2	
Car		Tax liability	
Car		Other	
Boat/Caravan/other			
Share of business			
Share of family trust			
Other			
TOTAL		TOTAL	

* Do not include funds held within superannuation

Total assets $_____ *less* Total liabilities $_____ = Net worth $_____

APPENDIX 3

10-YEAR PLAN

Time frame	Activity	Cost $
Short term: 1 to 2 years		
Medium term: 3 to 6 years		
Long term: 7 to 10 years		

APPENDIX 4

ANNUAL BUDGET

	JAN	FEB	MAR	APR	MAY	JUNE	JULY	AUG	SEP	OCT	NOV	DEC	TOTAL
INCOME													
Salary – H													
Salary – W													
Dividends/Interest													
Overtime/Bonus													
Other													
TOTAL													
EXPENDITURE													
FIXED													
Mortgage/rent													
Repayments – personal loan													
Repayments – credit card													
Repayments – other													

	JAN	FEB	MAR	APR	MAY	JUNE	JULY	AUG	SEP	OCT	NOV	DEC	TOTAL
Groceries													
Rates													
Insurance – Home													
Insurance – contents													
Insurance – car													
Insurance – other vehicles													
Insurance – health													
Insurance – personal													
Insurance – other													
Electricity													
Gas													
Solar													
Petrol													
Vehicle registration													
Vehicle maintenance													
Licence													
Donations													

	JAN	FEB	MAR	APR	MAY	JUNE	JULY	AUG	SEP	OCT	NOV	DEC	TOTAL
Gym/club memberships													
Subscriptions													
House cleaner													
Gardener													
Dry cleaning													
Regular savings													
REGULAR													
Clothing													
Taxis/public transport													
Furniture													
Appliances													
Home maintenance													
Chemist													
Medical costs													
Vet fees													
Bank fees													

	JAN	FEB	MAR	APR	MAY	JUNE	JULY	AUG	SEP	OCT	NOV	DEC	TOTAL
DISCRETIONARY													
Bank fees													
Gifts													
Entertainment													
Hobbies													
Takeaway food													
Sport													
Holidays													
Other													
TOTAL													
OVERSPEND													
UNDERSPEND													

APPENDIX 5

PERSONAL INSURANCE NEEDS ANALYSIS

Death and Total & Permanent Disability (TPD)

Immediate needs

Mortgage discharge/home provision

Investment property discharge

Other investment loans

Other outstanding debts

Education funding

Emergency income

Replacement items (e.g. motor vehicles)

Estate and funeral expenses

Subtotal

Income needs

Income for spouse

Income for children

Less expected investment returns

Subtotal

Realisable assets

Investment assets

Investment property

Life insurance (existing)

Superannuation

Subtotal

Summary

Immediate needs

Income needs

Total estate required

Less realisable assets

Estate shortfall

Cover required

Critical illness

Total outstanding debts

Emergency income

Medical and rehabilitation costs

Subtotal

Less existing cover

Cover required

Income protection

75% of monthly gross income

Less existing monthly income protection benefit

Required monthly income protection

How long could you survive without regular income?

For how long should the monthly benefit be paid?

INDEX

Index

Index